Religious Influences on Economic Thinking

Karl Brunner Distinguished Lecture Series

Nicolas Cuche-Curti and Lukas Voellmy, editors

John B. Taylor, *Reform of the International Monetary System: Why and How?*

Otmar Issing, *The Long Journey of Central Bank Communication*

Raghuram Rajan, *Monetary Policy and Its Discontents*

Benjamin M. Friedman, *Religious Influences on Economic Thinking: The Origins of Modern Economics*

Religious Influences on Economic Thinking

The Origins of Modern Economics

Benjamin M. Friedman

The MIT Press
Cambridge, Massachusetts
London, England

The MIT Press would like to thank the anonymous peer reviewers who provided comments on drafts of this book. The generous work of academic experts is essential for establishing the authority and quality of our publications. We acknowledge with gratitude the contributions of these otherwise uncredited readers.

This book was set in Stone Serif and Stone Sans by Jen Jackowitz. Printed and bound in the United States of America.

Library of Congress Cataloging-in-Publication Data

Names: Friedman, Benjamin M., author.
Title: Religious influences on economic thinking : the origins of modern economics / Benjamin M. Friedman.
Description: Cambridge, Massachusetts : The MIT Press, [2024] | Series: Karl Brunner distinguished lecture series | Includes bibliographical references and index.
Identifiers: LCCN 2023031886 (print) | LCCN 2023031887 (ebook) | ISBN 9780262548786 (paperback) | ISBN 9780262379403 (epub) | ISBN 9780262379410 (pdf)
Subjects: LCSH: Economics. | Economic development.
Classification: LCC HB171 .F765 2024 (print) | LCC HB171 (ebook) | DDC 330.1—dc23/eng/20231201
LC record available at https://lccn.loc.gov/2023031886
LC ebook record available at https://lccn.loc.gov/2023031887

10 9 8 7 6 5 4 3 2 1

In memory of Dan Bell and Bill Hutchison
Two Harvard greats

It is good advice to always study the preconceptions of a science.
—Paul Samuelson

Contents

Contents

Series Foreword

The Swiss National Bank is grateful to Benjamin Friedman for writing this book in which he revisits and develops the ideas presented in his Karl Brunner Distinguished Lecture of September 22, 2022. The series of books associated with the Karl Brunner Distinguished Lecture explores topics of key importance to central banking.

The Karl Brunner Distinguished Lecture Series, which is organized by the Swiss National Bank and takes place annually in Zurich, honors eminent monetary theory and policy thinkers whose research has influenced central banking. The scope of the series reflects the attention Karl Brunner devoted to monetary economics, his belief in the need to advance theoretical and applied analysis in this field, and in particular his concern for the policy relevance of economic science.

Thomas J. Jordan, Chairman of the Governing Board

Introduction: Ideas and Their Origins

The historian Edmund Morgan observed that it is impossible to know why people acted as they did.[1] It is even harder to know why they thought as they did. Yet the origins of ideas intrigue us nonetheless, especially when those ideas have far-reaching consequences. We naturally want to know where the central ideas that govern our lives came from: why they arose when, and where, they did, and how they captured the attention and attracted the adherence that they achieved.

Our ideas about economics are no exception. If John Maynard Keynes was right that "the world is ruled by little else" than the ideas of economists and political philosophers, we have a right to know what influences generated their thinking as well.[2] Most people today, at least in the Western world, simply take for granted that we organize the economic sphere of our lives primarily around private initiative channeled through some form of market activity. But where did that presumption come from? And how has it survived the numerous challenges—practical, political, above all moral—that those with concerns about this way of conducting our economic affairs have raised over a span of not just years but centuries?

In my recent book *Religion and the Rise of Capitalism*, I argued that our central ideas about economics were initially enabled in part by new and highly controversial lines of religious thinking in the English-speaking Protestant world of the eighteenth century, in which Adam Smith, David Hume, and their contemporaries lived and wrote.[3] Economists today are mostly unaware of these long-standing religious roots of our economic thinking. Nor, typically, is the interested general public particularly conscious of the bearing of religious thought on our public debate about economic policy issues. Worse yet, when such links are suggested, as they are from time to time, they are commonly misunderstood. But religious concepts—not the daily or annual cycle of religious observances in which many citizens participate, but the fundamental belief structure that is a central part of how they and others too understand the world in which we live—are deeply at work in shaping our thinking about many aspects of human life, the economic sphere included.

This influence of religious thinking on economic ideas was especially important at the very inception of modern Western economics: the crucial transition in thinking about what we now call "economics" (the word did not yet exist) that we associate with Smith and the other foundational figures of that time. As the philosopher and intellectual historian Thomas Kuhn has argued, it is mostly in a discipline's infancy that it is subject to influence from outside on its fundamental concepts, presumptions, and approaches.[4] In the time of Smith and Hume, economics was a new science; in effect, they created it. The openness of their thinking to external influence—including influence from the religious controversies of the day—was especially great.

But the matter is more than just an origins story. The influence of religious thinking on modern economic thinking at the field's inception established resonances that have persisted through the subsequent centuries, even as the economic context has evolved and the questions economists ask have shifted along with it, and likewise as the analytical and empirical tools at economists' disposal have expanded and improved. Because we are largely not conscious of these influences, neither in the past nor as they are at work today, we are sometimes puzzled when we stumble across evidence of their consequences—for example, in the otherwise hard-to-explain attitudes that many of our fellow citizens (Americans especially) express on questions of economic policy. But they are at work today as they were in the past, and understanding them can only enhance the capacity of the economics profession, as well as key institutions like central banks, to contribute to our ongoing public discussion of the important questions on which the discipline so usefully bears.

🌼

I am grateful to the Swiss National Bank, and especially to the chairman of the bank's governing board, Thomas Jordan, for inviting me to give this distinguished lecture in memory of my long-time friend Karl Brunner. Karl was a generation older than I, and I looked to him as a mentor as well as a friend. I learned enormously from him, and moreover at an early and therefore formative stage of my own journey in economics. I respected him, and I liked him.

Most economists today remember Karl Brunner as a titan in the field of monetary economics: a prolific contributor to monetary research, the leader of the Konstanz Seminar on Monetary Theory and Policy, and the founding editor of both the *Journal of Money, Credit and Banking* and the *Journal of Monetary Economics*. To be sure, he was all that. But there was also the Karl Brunner of the Interlaken Seminar on Analysis and Ideology. Karl was a man of powerful analytical insight but broad intellect as well. He published papers with titles like "Religion and the Social Order" and "The Perception of Man and the Conception of Society."[5] Late in his life he spoke fondly of having discussed theology with Frank Knight during his days at Chicago, and philosophy with Hans Reichenbach when he was at UCLA.[6] Karl was a serious intellectual in the most widely inquiring way. I believe he would have been gratified at the idea of a lecture, in his memory, on the subject of religious influences on modern economic thinking at the field's inception.

I am also grateful to President Joel Mesot of ETH for hosting this event. Zurich is a particularly appropriate place in which to discuss the ideas that I explore in this lecture. There were three important centers in the earliest days of the Protestant Reformation: Wittenberg, where Martin Luther lived and preached; Zurich, Huldrych Zwingli's home; and Geneva, where John Calvin dominated. Zwingli was almost an exact contemporary of Luther's, and the tension between the two pioneering thinkers was the stuff of intense debate until the end of Zwingli's short life.[7] And Calvin, who was a generation younger, did not arrive in Geneva, much less come to prominence, until after Zwingli's death. It is tantalizing to speculate on how the Reformation in Switzerland—which is the form of the Reformation that spread to the Netherlands and the English-speaking world—would have evolved had Zwingli not died in 1531.[8]

Moreover, many of the early events that were crucial to establishing the direction of the Reformation took place in or near Zurich.[9] The First Disputation of Zurich, in January 1523, one of the earliest public intellectual battles between the reformers and the Catholic Church, pitted Zwingli against

Johannes Fabri, at the time vicar general of Constance and later bishop of Vienna. The Zurich Bible, one of the first and most important translations of the holy scripture into the vernacular, was produced by a team of translators led by Zwingli and published in 1531 by Christoph Froschauer, Zurich's first printer (with woodcut illustrations by Hans Holbein the Younger).

Zurich was the scene of more disorderly episodes as well, and they too were important to the early course of the Reformation. In 1524, at Zwingli's behest, the Zurich magistrates ordered all religious images stripped from the city's churches. In the same year zealot reformers (they were not yet called "Protestants") stormed the Carthusian monastery at nearby Ittengen. In 1528 the Zurich authorities executed several Anabaptists by drowning them in the Limat. And in 1531 Zwingli—whose larger-than-life statue in Zurich today depicts him carrying both a book and a sword—was killed in battle, fighting for the Protestant side in the Second Kappel War.

Finally, I am also grateful to others who made this work possible: Lukas Voellmy of the Swiss National Bank, who oversaw my stay in Zurich with warm hospitality; Erik Nordbye and David Grant Smith, who provided essential research assistance; and the John Templeton Foundation and the Bowen H. and Janice Arthur McCoy Foundation, both of which supported the underlying research.

1 The "Economic" Problem

The centerpiece of modern economics, often labeled the First Fundamental Welfare Theorem, is the proposition that individuals, acting merely in their own self-interest in a competitive market setting, take actions that make not just themselves but also others better off. To newcomers not already immersed in this line of thinking, the idea often seems counterintuitive if not outright astonishing. Where did it come from?

Two profound inquiries, each of great antiquity, came together—something like opposing winds meeting to form a tornado, or vortex—to create the intellectual vacuum that Adam Smith ended up filling. The older inquiry concerned the proper role of self-interest in human behavior, and specifically the dangers of self-interested behavior carried to excess. What to think about self-interested behavior and what to do about it—the moral challenge as well as the practical problem—have been central to human thinking since mankind first began to commit thought to writing (and probably long before). Both the Hebrew Bible and the New Testament express a deep awareness of the temptations, and the dangers, associated with people looking out for themselves without regard for anyone else. In a different way, so did other early Middle Eastern texts

both religious and secular, and classical philosophers both
Stoic and Epicurean. The question likewise underlay much of
post-biblical Jewish and Christian moralizing. The tradition
of Renaissance humanism, hailing the republican virtues that
people of the time associated with ancient Greece and pre-
empire Rome, likewise addressed the need to put the polity
before one's self.

The subject was a particular focus of public concern in
Britain during the century or so leading up to Adam Smith's
time. Questions of civic virtue versus corruption—often with
an explicit link drawn between corruption and market-based
commerce—were a staple of debate throughout England's
Puritan revolution and then, after the parliamentary side's
victory in the English Civil War, under the republican Commonwealth.[1] The subsequent restoration of the monarchy
under Charles II, complete with the usual ostentatious luxury characteristic of European royal courts of the day, brought
a moral backlash against extravagant consumption together
with heightened concerns over the nation's moral character.[2]

The issue did not go away with Charles's death. After jointly
assuming the throne in the Glorious Revolution of 1688, William and Mary issued repeated proclamations against "vice,
immorality and corruption." In 1699 the Church of England
established the Society for Promoting Christian Knowledge, with much the same purpose in mind. In addition to
its missionary work abroad, at home in England the society
instituted charity schools to educate children in the usual
subjects of the day including religion and morality. Queen
Anne, who ascended to the throne on William's death in 1702
(Mary had predeceased him), in turn issued a Proclamation
for the Encouragement of Piety and Virtue and for the Pre-
venting and Punishing of Vice, Profaneness and Immorality.

But concern over public morality was more than a matter of frustrated authority at the top. Starting in the 1690s, private Societies for the Reformation of Manners emerged, in London and other towns, to enforce moral discipline by informing on their neighbors' misdeeds: sexual misbehavior, drunkenness, gambling, profanity, even merely failing to observe the Sabbath. These voluntary groups had limited success, however, and within a few decades this effort too collapsed.[3]

The economic dimension of the era's perceived vice and immorality took on particular visibility after 1720, with the bursting of the South Sea Bubble, one of financial history's classic episodes of speculation followed by collapse, comparable to the Dutch tulip mania a century before and to numerous well-known shakeouts of market excess since. The South Sea Company fiasco also became an emblem of corruption on a grand scale. The astonishing run-up in the company's share price turned out to have involved stock manipulation, inside dealing, fanciful touting of the company's earnings prospects, and lending to investors on the security of current holdings to finance purchases of still more shares. It also emerged that key members of Parliament had taken bribes in return for promoting the venture at the outset. But the South Sea Company was hardly unique; other unscrupulous promoters were carrying out similar schemes, engaging in many of the same forms of manipulation, on a smaller scale.

The subject was a principal focus of intellectual discourse as well. Spurred by the trauma of the Reformation and then the English Civil War—and on the continent the Thirty Years' War, the Spanish-Dutch Conflict and numerous other hostilities— much of the political discussion of issues of vice and virtue in Britain, at the end of the seventeenth century and beginning of the eighteenth, reflected memories of the cruelty and death that these conflicts had brought, and the intolerance, fanaticism, and persecution that had stood behind them. The discussion centered on the question of man's "sociability," or lack of it, and the implications that followed for whether, and if so how, human societies could govern themselves.[4] The ever-increasing complexity and anonymity of the market society in which these thinkers lived further compounded this challenge.

The economic sphere was perhaps the most obvious arena in which everyday behavior by ordinary men and women revolved around self-interest. Further, the question of the proper role for individual self-interest that economic inter-action posed only grew in importance as Britain's economy, still mostly agricultural, evolved toward an ever-greater role for commercial markets. Most farmers now looked to markets, and increasingly so, for their economic existence. Even tenants who farmed on lords' estates relied on shopkeepers and goods purveyors of all kinds to supply their daily necessities. Trades-men and townspeople were in most cases entirely dependent on market interactions, acting both as sellers of whatever they produced and buyers of whatever they needed. By the end of the seventeenth century, the challenge surrounding self-interest importantly included seeking to understand the social basis underlying what was becoming an increasingly commercialized economy. Especially in the arena of economic life, overcoming the dangers posed by self-interest seemed an insurmountable challenge.

❧

The other long-standing inquiry that contributed to setting the stage for the creation of modern Western economics concerned how to organize the producing and consuming, the buying and selling, that made up so much of everyday life.

For centuries, practically oriented lines of thought had largely taken for granted that economic activity was best directed by some form of higher authority. By the latter half of the seventeenth century, the French had advanced top-down dirigisme to new heights under the "mercantilist" system developed by Louis XIV's finance minister, Jean-Baptiste Colbert. The English, more in patchwork fashion, had developed an elaborate system of government-granted monopolies restricting who could produce what.

What was new in this inquiry in Adam Smith's day was explicit concern for *economic* welfare. Until roughly the time of Smith and his contemporaries, there was little consensus that aggregate economic welfare in today's sense of a society's standard of living was a subject to think much about at all. There was even less consensus that anyone could do much about it. In biblical times people had understood that economic conditions could be good or bad, but they mostly attributed the difference to two influences: plentiful versus meager harvests, and war versus peace. In a mostly agrarian economy the harvest was naturally of paramount importance, but there was little room for economic initiative to affect it. The Bible's view of the matter was that good harvest conditions were instead a reward for proper moral and religious behavior. Similarly, though surely not for this reason only, hopes for peace were a biblical centerpiece.

Both the early Christian fathers and the scholastics of the Middle Ages likewise took little interest in what might enhance a society's material living standard. Their focus was not on this world but the life to come. Economic behavior mattered, but mostly because the individual acts that comprised it could potentially be sinful, and therefore might impede an individual soul's salvation. From the viewpoint of the society as a whole, what mattered was not the standard of living, which presumably no one could influence anyway, but whether people's economic interactions were channeled according to religious principles. Buying and selling were accepted, as long as the price was "just." So were individual borrowing and lending, but only if no interest was charged.[5] Further, in the eyes of the church improving the general standard of living was not necessarily desirable even if it were somehow possible.

The Renaissance took a different direction, idealizing the aristocratic pursuit of honor and glory. What the thinkers of the day considered glorious, however, was not anything to do with mass living standards but instead sumptuous display by princes and their hangers-on, together with the public monuments—palaces, churches, fountains, gardens—that they built. Honor and glory for princes also came from military adventures. A society's productive capacity mattered because it potentially enabled construction of monuments and the manufacture of weapons (and, when needed, the hiring of mercenaries), not on account of any direct benefit to the general population. In Europe, the resulting subordination of economic activity to "reasons of state" reached new heights in seventeenth-century France under Louis XIV.

The standard mercantilist economic program promoted domestic manufacturing, especially of products likely to appeal to export markets, and in parallel discouraged imports—all in order to accumulate and retain gold and silver bullion. Not by accident, such policies were far from neutral in whom they favored. A monopoly over some good's production, or its sale, protected the interest of whoever received the royal license and blocked anyone else who might seek to enter that line of business. The sale of monopolies also provided a much-needed source of revenue for the king. Over time, therefore, the "reasons of state" behind such policies became conflated with the interest of producers. By contrast, the public's consumption at best absorbed goods that might be sold abroad, and sometimes required imported goods, which had to be paid for. A further element of the mercantilist program, therefore, was to keep wages, and hence the population's standard of living, low. More generally, mercantilist policies required top-down implementation, involving a profusion of state-granted monopolies and state-imposed restrictions on trade.

It was not until the eighteenth century, primarily in England and even more so in Scotland, that thinking about economic questions began to focus on improving a nation's overall standard of living. The Scots' desire to gain access to England's colonial trade, and thereby achieve a level of economic development comparable to what the English already enjoyed, was the principal motivation for entering into the Act of Union with England in 1707. Abolishing their country's parliament, and for most practical purposes its royal court as well, was bound to be controversial. It is not surprising, therefore, that it was in Scotland, and in the decades following the Act of Union, that the concept of a nation's standard of living and the objective of improving it entered economic thinking in more or less the form we know today. David Hume, writing at midcentury, constructed the most penetrating rejection of mercantilist ideas on international trade, especially the obsession with accumulating gold and silver. Hume explained that increases in a country's holdings of specie would raise the prices of its goods, thereby undoing much of what the mercantilists hoped to achieve through a positive trade balance.[6] He also showed how, once thinking moved past the viewpoint of military rivalry, prosperity among a country's foreign competitors was beneficial not just to those other countries but at home too: greater wealth abroad meant greater foreign demand for home-produced goods.[7]

The understanding that the route to wealth was to trade with other nations—rather than to conquer them, and then plunder their riches and enslave their populations—was only just dawning on Europeans' thinking, and Hume's theory of international trade reflected it.[8] Adam Smith further elaborated the idea of trade as the avenue to prosperity and made even more explicit the objective of improving a country's general standard of living. The title of Smith's great work, *The Wealth of Nations*, referred to living standards, not holdings of gold and silver. What he wrote was, in effect, a guidebook for policymakers seeking to take a country from a low state of economic development like Scotland's to a more prosperous level like England's. Throughout, Smith was clear about the primary goal. "No society can surely be flourishing and happy," he declared, "of which the far greater part of the members are poor and miserable." What mostly mattered was "the condition of the labouring poor, of the great body of the people."[9] The question he took on was how to improve it.

2   The Competitive Market Mechanism

Three basic ideas encompassed much of "economic" thinking (the word did not yet exist in its current meaning) as of the beginning of the eighteenth century. First, in line with prevailing mercantilist practice, the presumption was that most individuals were probably not capable of perceiving what actions in the economic sphere were in their own self-interest; except in the very basics, they needed to be told what to do. Second, and more directly relevant to what in time became the First Fundamental Welfare Theorem, there was no sense that individuals acting in their self-interest, whether perceived correctly or not, would thereby make anyone other than themselves better off. And third—for just that reason, but also in keeping with much of traditional religious and moral thinking—action in the economic sphere motivated by self-interest was deemed morally opprobrious; in the standard language of the day, such behavior was a "vice," and the usual adjective applied to it was "vicious."

A century later all three presumptions were different: Most individuals probably could perceive what economic actions were in their self-interest. (At least they could when they acted as *producers* of goods and services; Adam Smith, for example, was scathing on the foolish behavior of individuals in their role as consumers, especially the rich.) Individuals acting in their own self-interest could—and under the right conditions they *would*—end up making others better off too. And acting in one's self-interest, at least in the economic sphere, was no longer deemed morally opprobrious. (The words "vice" and "vicious" do appear in Smith's two books—but never referring merely to self-interested behavior.) On all three counts, the principal impetus driving the change was the contribution of Adam Smith.

Born in 1723 to an educated though hardly prosperous family in the village of Kirkcaldy, across the Firth of Forth from Edinburgh, Smith attended the local parish school and at age fourteen entered the university at Glasgow.[1] At age seventeen he took up a scholarship at Balliol College, Oxford, where he remained for six years. No doubt he used the time to read extensively, and to think about what he read. But he produced no serious writings of his own during these years, and he left little record of what he read or what he thought. He apparently found scant intellectual stimulation from either the dons or his fellow students during these years.

Returning home in 1746, Smith soon came to the attention of Edinburgh's intellectual elite. Through the patronage of Henry Home, Lord Kames, a wealthy Scottish lawyer and also a prominent thinker about government and politics (and very distantly related to David Hume), Smith received a commission to deliver two sets of public lectures: one on rhetoric, the other on jurisprudence. The lectures, which he presented in Edinburgh between 1748 and 1751, provided him an opportunity to begin work on the project, inspired by Hume, of building a systematic scientific study of human behavior comparable to what Newton had achieved for the physical world. Although he did not publish what he wrote at the time, aspects of Smith's later thinking, including parts of *The Wealth of Nations* as well as a course of lectures that he taught at Glasgow (not published until long after his death), seem to have taken their initial shape from these early public lectures in Edinburgh. The lectures also enhanced Smith's reputation and visibility in Scottish intellectual circles, enough so that when the professorship of logic and metaphysics at Glasgow fell vacant, in late 1750, Smith was elected. Soon after, however, the professorship of moral philosophy became vacant, and the following spring Smith was elected to that position instead. At age twenty-nine, he now occupied what had been his admired teacher Francis Hutcheson's chair.

The chief product of Smith's years of teaching at Glasgow was *The Theory of Moral Sentiments*, published in 1759. Drawing on his training in Stoic philosophy, insights he had taken from Hume (the central role of the human imagination, for example), and ideas he had absorbed from Francis Hutcheson (human "sympathy," for example, which Smith highlighted in the very first sentence, and the desire for "fellow feeling" as well as both self-respect and the respect of others), the book laid out a theory of interpersonal relationships that indirectly underpinned the view of markets that he went on to lay out, a decade and a half later, in *The Wealth of Nations*. (Most obviously, the ability of producers of goods and services to anticipate what potential customers would want to buy, and thereby know what to make and offer for sale, depends on the imaginative capacity to "put oneself in others' shoes.") But *The Theory of Moral Sentiments* was more than that, and its fully developed theory of human relations at both the individual and societal level established Smith's reputation as a philosopher internationally as well as at home.

In 1764, at the age of forty-one, Smith resigned his university position at Glasgow to accept an appointment as tutor and traveling companion to a young Scottish nobleman, and from February of that year until October 1766, the two traveled together—first to Toulouse, then Geneva, and finally Paris. Living for two and a half years in these intellectual centers on the continent gave Smith, who was already widely known as the author of *The Theory of Moral Sentiments*, an opportunity to exchange ideas at first hand with many of the leading thinkers of the French Enlightenment. The most influential of these new contacts for Smith's subsequent thinking was François Quesnay, the leading figure in a school of French thinkers known as "physiocrats" for their emphasis on land and agriculture as the sole source of economic wealth. Smith found this narrow focus on agriculture unpersuasive, but some of the physiocrats' ideas—especially Quesnay's systematic way of thinking about the interrelatedness of different elements of a nation's economy—significantly influenced his thinking.[2] (He later said that if Quesnay had lived to see the publication of *The Wealth of Nations*, he would have dedicated the book to his French friend.[3])

It was apparently during his stay in Toulouse that Smith began to write the book that became *The Wealth of Nations*.[4] After returning from France in 1766, he devoted most of the next nine years to working on it. While he paid close attention to ongoing economic and political events, and what he wrote partly reflected these contemporary concerns, the main practical impetus to his thinking remained the challenge that had driven Scotland to give up its independence at the very beginning of the century: how to increase economic activity and make it more productive, so as to improve everyday living standards for ordinary working people. By the middle of the eighteenth century, it seemed that nearly everything the state tried to do in the economic sphere was at best unnecessary and more likely counterproductive. At the same time, the material progress that was now visibly occurring sprang mostly from individual initiative and owed little to the direction of the state.[5] Mercantilism was clearly not any kind of solution. But rejecting state intervention, after centuries of reliance on government-granted monopolies, licenses, and other restrictions, would represent a wholesale change in thinking. Making a persuasive case for such a shift would require a sound theoretical foundation.

Smith's route to meeting this challenge encompassed several key elements. First, reaffirming the stance he had taken in *The Theory of Moral Sentiments*, he asserted that the desire to improve our material living standard is innate in humans, and therefore no more morally opprobrious than the fact that we need to eat and breathe. "The desire of bettering our condition," he now wrote, "comes with us from the womb, and never leaves us till we go into the grave. In the whole interval which separates those two moments, there is scarce perhaps a single instant in which any man is . . . without any wish of alteration or improvement."[6] Although in his earlier book Smith had pointed to Stoic "tranquility" as the route to human happiness, he nonetheless now recognized that constant restlessness and material striving more nearly characterized human existence. Moreover, while "bettering our condition" could in principle refer to any of a variety of dimensions of human life, Smith was clear that the condition most people seek to better is their *economic* condition: "An augmentation of fortune is the means by which the greater part of men . . . wish to better their condition."[7] As a philosopher he might still prefer that people seek tranquility and enjoyment from society and conversation; but he saw *The Wealth of Nations* as science, not sermonizing—as both Hume and Rousseau had put it, taking men as they are—and he now simply accepted as an observed fact that most people are intent on improving their material well-being.

Smith also assumed that the economic world he was addressing was one of "commerce"—by which he meant the combination of specialized production and voluntary exchange—and his observations on this form of economic organization made up a large part of the new book's lasting contribution. Just as *The Theory of Moral Sentiments* had begun with an assertion of the universal prevalence of human sympathy, the very first sentence of *The Wealth of Nations* trumpeted the advantages of specialization in production—"division of labor," as Smith called it.[8] The opening paragraph of the second chapter then tied specialized production to voluntary exchange. Much of the rest of the book can be read as an elaboration of the role of these two crucial features of what he and his contemporaries meant by commerce.

What was new in *The Wealth of Nations*—and what made the book so important, then and now—was Smith's sophisticated understanding of competition conducted within markets as the principal organizing mechanism of economic activity carried out under commerce. His analysis centered on the dynamic role played by prices, including wages as the price of labor services. Smith did not work out mathematically the joint interaction of supply and demand. That came a hundred years later, with Alfred Marshall. But he clearly understood, and carefully explained, the several functions that prices serve: as reflections of scarcity, enabling consumers to buy more of cheap goods while forcing them to hold back on expensive ones; as incentives to production, motivating craftsmen and manufacturers to make more of some goods and less of others; and as guides to allocation, steering scarce and therefore expensive resources toward uses in which they are more highly valued, while allowing more plentiful and therefore cheaper resources to be used in less valuable ways. Today these roles played by prices are central to even the most basic understanding of Western economics. In *The Wealth of Nations*, they were new.

Most important, Smith grounded the mechanism of price determination on nothing more than buyers' and sellers' pursuit of their respective self-interest. What led these buyers and sellers to the price that fully reflected the scarcity of the goods being produced and the cost of the labor and material inputs used to produce them, steering production to the right goods and the best techniques for making them, was the way they and other participants in markets compete among themselves, with no more than their respective self-interest in mind. The same principle, always grounded in market competition together with the self-interest of the parties on opposite sides of the buy-sell transaction, was at work again and again, in one setting after another. The outcome was a striking example of the closely related Enlightenment-era principles of unintended consequences and spontaneous order, and Smith repeatedly emphasized that far from intending the benefits to others that resulted from their own actions, the participants in the process did not even foresee them. True, human beings have sympathy for one another, as he had argued at length in *The Theory of Moral Sentiments*, but that sympathy is not what was at work here. And even if people were disposed to advance others' economic well-being, Smith did not want his version of a Newtonian "system" to have to depend on their having sufficient knowledge to be able to do so.

With this insight, Smith finally had the key to the para-
dox posed by thinkers like the Frenchman Pierre Nicole and
the Dutch-born Bernard Mandeville, beginning more than a
century before: it was self-interest, *operating through the market
mechanism*, that led each of the "bees" in Mandeville's much
discussed *Fable* to satisfy the others' desires and therefore,
taken all together, to make their "hive" prosper. In Nicole's
vocabulary, no "charity" was necessary. As Smith concluded,
in what became one of the most frequently quoted passages in
The Wealth of Nations: "It is not from the benevolence of the
butcher, the brewer, or the baker, that we expect our dinner,
but from their regard to their own interest. We address our-
selves, not to their humanity but to their self-love, and never
talk to them of our own necessities but of their advantages."[9]
Market competition was the mechanism behind the benefit to
others created by our pursuing our self-interest, and the price
system was how market competition worked. Channeled
through competition carried out in markets, and operating
through the effect of that competition on prices, the effort of
each individual to do no more than improve his own condition was "the principle from which publick and national, as
well as private opulence is originally derived."[10]

Here, at last, was the secret to what has come down to us
as the First Fundamental Welfare Theorem—and what both
economists and the general public, ever since, have understood as the "invisible hand" (even though Smith did not specifically use the famous metaphor in this section of the book).
Even as both parties to an economic transaction vied against
one another, and even though each was pursuing his or her
own interest only, under the right conditions *both* would
benefit, as would others as well. In modern terms, economic
relations—again, under the right conditions—are not zero-sum.

In contrast to Hume, who had stated that people's interest in acquiring goods and possessions is "directly destructive of society," Smith now showed how market competition enabled the universal effort to better one's condition via an "augmentation of fortune" to advance living standards more broadly, and even foster human sociability.[11] Others, like Pierre Nicole and Pierre de Boisguilbert in France and then Bernard Mandeville and Josiah Tucker in England, had grasped that self-interested behavior could promote the common good. But it was Smith who explained how market competition made it so.

In keeping with Smith's objective in writing his great book, the principle of positive but unintended benefits stemming from self-interest harnessed by market competition had not just descriptive power but normative force too. In the absence of perpetually ongoing technical progress, which he did not foresee (he lived a half-century too early to grasp the driving force of the Industrial Revolution), the only way Smith thought an economically advanced country could continue to improve its productivity and hence its standard of living was to keep increasing the degree of specialization—division of labor—with which it produced ordinary goods and services. But a country starting off with an insufficiently developed system of markets, or with adequate markets but a host of government-imposed monopolies and other bars to competition within them, could achieve a *once-for-all* productivity gain by eliminating these impediments.

Smith was sharply critical, therefore, not only of mercantilist systems like what he had observed in France but also of the many forms of economic restrictions then in place in England and Scotland. In *The Wealth of Nations* he set forth at length his opposition to mercantilism, beginning from the "popular notion"—which he showed to be false—"that wealth consists in money, or in gold and silver." He went on to explain, with copious historical detail, the failure of the policies to which pursuit of this end frequently led. More fundamentally, he argued that while "consumption is the sole end and purpose of all production," so that the interest of the producer is worth promoting only to the extent necessary for achieving better outcomes for consumers, under mercantilism the opposite orientation dominates: "In the mercantile system, the interest of the consumer is almost constantly sacrificed to that of the producer; and it seems to consider production, and not consumption, as the ultimate end and object of all industry and commerce."[12] To Smith, such thinking was simply backward.

At a more specific level—referring now to England and Scotland—Smith opposed local customs taxes as well as either taxes or outright prohibitions on imports from abroad (in each case in order to allow freer flow of goods); traditional guild-enforced apprenticeship regulations (freer allocation of labor); government-granted monopolies (freer choice of what to produce and who could produce it); and entails and other restrictions on property transfers (freer ownership, and therefore allocation, of land). Writing about Britain's colonies in America and the Caribbean, he opposed slavery. Smith intended his book as a practical guide for raising a country's standard of living. Allowing market competition to function naturally, as people's inborn desire for economic gain and propensity for trade propelled them, was the most effective way to achieve that end.

Smith also recognized that government is not the only source of harmful impediments to competition. On just the same grounds that he opposed state monopolies and licenses, he was blunt in his criticism of attempts by merchants and manufacturers to monopolize markets or otherwise band together to force prices higher or wages lower. In Glasgow and Edinburgh, and probably in London too during his extended stays there, he had observed merchants and other employers sufficiently closely to become skeptical of their motives and their methods. The popular image of Smith as an advocate of free markets is correct, but today's frequent representation of him as therefore a supporter of whatever private businesses seek to do is not. Merchants, he wrote, constitute "an order of men . . . who have generally an interest to deceive and even to oppress the publick, and who accordingly have, upon many occasions both deceived and oppressed it."[13]

But notwithstanding the harm that he associated with impediments to competition created by either government or the collusion of businessmen, and the gains that he argued a country could reap by eliminating them both, Smith nonetheless emphasized not the fragility of the market mechanism he had identified but instead its astonishing robustness. Because of this strong confidence in the positive force of markets, he was never the rigid opponent of all regulation that many political conservatives today hold him out to be. He favored tight restrictions on banking (tighter than in any Western country today) in order to prevent financial crises and consequent economic collapse like what Scotland had experienced in 1772, and he favored public education (less comprehensive than what we have today, but well beyond what England in particular had then) as a way to overcome the dulling effect on the human intellect that he feared from the ever-advancing division of labor.

In the same vein, he also advocated progressive income taxes, on straightforward distributional grounds ("It is not very unreasonable that the rich should contribute to the publick expence, not only in proportion to their revenue, but something more than in that proportion"); heavier highway tolls on luxury carriages, likewise on distributional grounds (so that "the indolence and vanity of the rich is made to contribute in a very easy manner to the relief of the poor"); taxes on the retail sale of liquor, and especially heavy taxes on distilleries (despite living in Scotland!); and, of course, taxes on any kind of monopoly profit ("the gains of monopolists, whenever they can be come at, [are] certainly of all subjects the most proper" for taxation).[14]

In contrast to the view among many economists and political figures today that a market economy is such a delicate piece of machinery that any interference—especially one aimed at achieving more equitable outcomes—will seriously undermine it, Smith thought the power of self-interest, at work in competitive markets, was sufficient to overcome most obstacles that either government or colluding businessmen created. "The natural effort of every individual to better his own condition," he wrote, "is so powerful a principle, that it is alone, and without any assistance, not only capable of carrying on the society to wealth and prosperity, but of surmounting a hundred impertinent obstructions with which the folly of human laws too often incumbers its operations." No classic republican sense of virtue, in which individuals willingly subordinate their self-interest to the common good, is involved. All that is necessary is "the natural system of perfect liberty and justice." The force of self-interest, operating in competitive markets, is "frequently powerful enough to maintain the natural progress of things toward improvement, in spite of the extravagance of government, and of the greatest errors of administration."[15] He not only accepted the First Fundamental Welfare Theorem. With his theory of competitive markets he explained why, and under what conditions, it was so.

✹

With *The Wealth of Nations*, Adam Smith assumed the place in the forefront of Enlightenment thinkers that he has held ever since. The book attracted immediate acclaim, both in England and Scotland and in foreign translations. Especially following the set of public lectures based on the book, given in 1800–1801 by Dugald Stewart, then the professor of moral philosophy at the University of Edinburgh, it rose to a heightened level of prominence that it has retained for more than two centuries.

More important, with *The Wealth of Nations* the fundamental basis of what we now call "economics" was established. According to Donald Winch, probably the foremost Adam Smith scholar of our generation, the book became "the fountain-head of classical political economy."[16] It has served as the fundamental source of modern economic thinking as well. The role of market competition has remained the discipline's central conceptual apparatus. Much of the field's development since then has involved working out in greater depth and sophistication just how market competition works, and what consequences ensue when it fails to do so. In one Western country after another, much of the surrounding policy debate has likewise turned on how to enable competitive markets to do their job, and what to do when they can't. Adam Smith—not any of his predecessors, valuable as their contributions may have been—is rightly known as the father of modern economics.

3   The Sunset of Orthodox Calvinism

What enabled Smith to come to these powerful insights? To be sure, he had learned from others who came before. From his time in France, he knew the market-oriented work of Pierre de Boisguilbert and also Richard Cantillon, whose book *Essay on the Nature of Trade* had then been recently published and was receiving much attention at the time of Smith's visit. He had spent decades pondering the challenge posed by Mandeville, and he knew the responses—from Hutcheson, Hume, and many others—that Mandeville's deliberately shocking way of presenting his ideas had provoked. Although there is no direct evidence on the matter, he also presumably knew Nicole's essay on the outward resemblance of charity and self-love.[1] And there were contemporary and recent economic thinkers in Britain whose work he knew as well: not only his friend and mentor Hume but also Adam Ferguson, professor of moral philosophy (before Dugald Stewart) at Edinburgh; Joseph Butler, bishop of Bristol and later of Durham, and also dean of St. Paul's in London; Butler's protégé Josiah Tucker, dean of Gloucester, who like Smith thought of the economy as a kind of self-regulating mechanism and therefore wrote in opposition to mercantilism and other market restrictions; Sir James Steuart, a fellow Scot who, unlike Smith, favored top-down economic systems and called for better public management of the economy; and more besides.

Smith's education and experience mattered too. The presumption of a harmony in nature stemming from the inherent rationality and order of the universe, which he had absorbed from studying the Stoics, was fully consistent with the belief that natural human desires and proclivities, left alone, led to beneficial outcomes that no one either anticipated or intended. Nature was fully compatible with reason, and human instincts with rational designs.[2] From this perspective, both government regulation and private monopoly represented corruption of the natural order.[3] Even the invisible hand metaphor was a familiar Stoic motif, compactly expressing the principle of unintended consequences and emblematic of the harmonious convergence of natural tendencies and what reason would choose.

The legacy of Isaac Newton was an especially powerful influence. Newton's monumental *Principia Mathematica* had been published in 1687, and by Smith's day it was part of the standard undergraduate curriculum at all four Scottish universities as well as at Cambridge in England (interestingly, however, not at Oxford—which may help explain why Oxford lagged behind for so long in scientific studies). For a generation of intellectuals educated in Newtonian concepts of system and mechanism, intuiting an outcome without being able to explain it—in this case, being able to state the First Fundamental Welfare Theorem without knowing why it was true—was not adequate. When thinkers like Smith and Hume turned their attention to the economic or political sphere, their goal, stated in the broadest terms, was to construct a science of man comparable to what Newton had achieved for the physical world.

Even the language that Smith used in his account of the market mechanism had a strikingly Newtonian flavor. Explaining how a market for any good maintains its price at the level that renders supply equal to demand, Smith wrote that what he called the "natural price"—what today we think of as the market-clearing equilibrium price—is "the central price, to which the prices of all commodities are continually *gravitating*. Different accidents may sometimes keep them *suspended* a good deal above it, and sometimes *force* them down even somewhat below it. But whatever may be the obstacles which hinder them from *settling* in this center of repose and continuance, they are constantly tending towards it."[4] He could just as well have been writing about planets settling into their orbits.

And too, parts of Smith's analysis reflected his close observation of the many aspects of economic activity he had encountered, from village life in Kirkaldy to mercantile bustle in Edinburgh, Glasgow, and London, and including what he saw when he visited France and Switzerland. These experiences often served to ground his more specific generalizations about how different economic actors behaved under various circumstances.

But even these influences hardly seem sufficient to account for the astonishing intellectual breakthrough that Smith achieved with *The Wealth of Nations*. Something else was at work as well, shaping the shared worldview that not only channeled his thinking but also made his contemporaries so willing to accept his insights once he presented them.

❀

The momentous change that Adam Smith and his contemporaries effected in thinking about human prospects in the economic realm was not the only intellectual groundswell under way in their society during their time. Religious thinking was undergoing a profound shift as well. The Protestant revolt against the Roman Catholic Church, which had begun in Germany under the impetus of Martin Luther, two centuries before Smith was born, had largely reached a mature stability by his adult lifetime. The respectively Protestant and Catholic areas of Europe were by then approximately what they are today. By contrast, the struggle over what Protestants thought about the essential questions that any religion faces was still very much in progress. It was especially so within the English-speaking world.

Three fundamental questions stood at the debate's center. First, what is the moral essence of human nature? Are humans, as a consequence of the sin of Adam and Eve in the Garden of Eden, "utterly depraved"—meaning that they are unable on their own to make moral choices and act in a moral way? Or did God, in creating our species, endow the human character with an inherent goodness that survived Adam's transgression, such that any man or woman, with the right encouragement and teaching, can aspire to a morally upright life and potentially achieve it?

Second, what becomes of humans after death? And if individual men and women's spiritual destinies differ, what determines those different paths? Is anyone potentially eligible for salvation, or only some? If it is only some—and maybe only a few—what determines who is saved and who isn't? In particular, do people's own choices and actions matter to this end? Or are individuals "predestined" so that some inevitably achieve salvation while others, just as inevitably, not only do not but cannot?

And third, why do humans exist in the first place? For religious believers, at a time before Darwin, the answer was of course that humans exist because God created them. But to what end? For God's own glorification? For some other purpose? Whatever the purpose, does human happiness matter for it? More than that, is human happiness a, perhaps even *the*, divine intent for our kind?

The debate over the human character, although in this instance carried out among Christians, stemmed from the creation narrative in the Hebrew Bible, and in particular the sin of Adam and Eve that resulted in their being driven from the Garden of Eden. Augustine, the late-fourth- and early-fifth-century bishop perhaps best known today for his searing autobiographical *Confessions*, charted what became for centuries the dominant Christian view. God, he wrote, "created man righteous." Because the "seminal nature" from which all humans were to be propagated already existed in Adam, however, by Adam's sin the entire human race was "depraved in its origin, as from a corrupt root."[5] Left to themselves, humans were incapable of doing good. Luther likewise regarded a negative assessment of the human character as an essential part of a believer's faith. John Calvin, the principal thinker behind the Protestant movement in countries like Switzerland and the Netherlands—and soon in England and Scotland too—adhered even more closely to Augustine's harsh view of the human character. In his reading, the "miserable ruin, into which the rebellion of the first man cast us" implied "ignorance, vanity, poverty, infirmity and—what is more—depravity and corruption," not just of Adam and Eve themselves but also of all men and women after them. Calvin went on to define original sin, which all humans acquired from Adam, as "a hereditary depravity and corruption of our nature, diffused into all parts of the soul." Nor was original sin a matter of our being punished for what was merely our ancestors' error. "This is not liability for another's transgression," Calvin insisted. "We through his transgression have become entangled in the curse . . . not only has punishment fallen upon us from Adam, but a contagion imparted by him resides in us."[6]

The notion of humans' inborn depravity had implications beyond the realm of theology, however. It provided an explanation for humans' harmful, even disastrous, behavior toward one another, which persisted incorrigibly from one generation to the next. It bore a particular resonance for Europeans who had lived through the destruction and cruel atrocities of the Thirty Years' War and the English Civil War. Secular thinkers concerned with the limits to human sociability, and the challenge they posed to governance, likewise framed their inquiry in these terms. For Thomas Hobbes, the potential war of all against all was the greatest threat presented by fallen man. Adam Smith, following his teacher Francis Hutcheson, saw markets as an institution that disciplined individual behavior and that provided at least limited justice in the face of human imperfection.

Belief in Calvin's view of depravity and original sin acquired increasing dominance within English Protestantism. The *Thirty-nine Articles* of the Anglican Church followed Calvin closely in declaring that original sin (also called birth-sin) "standeth not in the following of Adam . . . it is the fault and corruption of the nature of every man." Man is "of his own nature inclined to evil."[7] Nearly a century later, at the high tide of orthodox Calvinist influence, *The Westminster Confession of Faith*, agreed upon by a gathering of Puritan theologians convened by Parliament during the English Civil War, declared, "Our first parents . . . sinned in eating the forbidden fruit . . . and so became dead in sin." And what implication followed for Adam and Eve's descendants? "They being the root of all mankind, the guilt of this sin was imputed, and the same death in sin and corrupted nature conveyed to all their posterity." The continuing implications for human character were severe: "From this original corruption . . . we are utterly indisposed, disabled, and made opposite to all good, and wholly inclined to do all evil."[8]

In light of this inherently sinful and corrupted nature of all humans—even newborn infants—what were Protestants to think about their individual prospects for ultimate salvation? Did the depravity so forcefully articulated by Calvin, and reconfirmed by the *Thirty-nine Articles* and then the *Westminster Confession*, condemn everyone to eternal damnation? If instead some are to be saved, then who? And by what means? Above all, for believers who are understandably concerned for their own ultimate spiritual prospects, can *any*body gain access to those means? And if so, how?

On this question the Hebrew Bible was mostly silent, as were the gospels of the New Testament. It was Paul, not the gospelists, who elaborated the sense in which only few are chosen. In his letter to the Romans, often considered his most important work, the apostle pondered whether God had turned away from the people of Israel. "Hath God cast away his people?" Paul asked. "God forbid," he answered. "At this present time also there is a remnant according to the election of grace." But the conclusion that the choice of this remnant was by grace bore an important implication: "if by grace, then it is no more of works; otherwise grace is no more grace."[9] Paul repeated the point in his letter to the Ephesians: "by grace ye are saved through faith, and that not of yourselves: it is the gift of God: not of works."[10] For this purpose God acted purely out of his own grace. Salvation could not be earned.

Beyond emphasizing the crucial role of God's grace, Paul also introduced the parallel idea of *pre*destination: that since an individual's election did not depend on his or her actions, God could—and did—make the choice to confer grace not only without waiting to see how the person lived but before the person even lived at all. Writing to the Ephesians, Paul explained that God's choice predated not only the individual's life but even the creation of the world: "He hath chosen us in him before the foundation of the world, that we should be holy and without blame before him." Even before creating the world, God had "predestinated us . . . according to the good pleasure of his will, to the praise of the glory of his grace, wherein he hath made us accepted in the beloved."[11]

The early church fathers, especially Augustine, likewise regarded predestination to salvation as a consequence of God's gift, which God "foreknew" that he would give to his chosen ones. Rejecting the possibility of human agency being effective for this purpose, Augustine too echoed Paul's disclaimer that this gift was in any respect bestowed in anticipation of an individual's own worth or deeds. Rather, it is "the true grace of God, that is, that which is not given in respect of our merits."[12] Eleven centuries later, Calvin elevated the doctrine of predestination, in the sense of both Paul and Augustine, to a place of paramount importance in his theology. With predestination, salvation—for those who were saved—was eternally secure; it was not contingent on human action. Moreover, Calvin was explicit about an aspect of the doctrine that Paul had left unspecified: "salvation is freely offered to some while others are barred from access to it." Some are to enjoy eternal life, others to suffer eternal damnation. God "does not indiscriminately adopt all into the hope of salvation but gives to some what he denies to others." Indeed, "by his just and irreprehensible but incomprehensible judgment he has barred the door of life to those whom he has given over to damnation."[13] Crucially, Calvin strictly followed both Paul and Augustine in attributing the choice to save or to damn a person to God's own grace, not the person's actions.

Here too, official belief among the early English Protestants followed Calvin's thinking. The *Thirty-nine Articles* stated, "Predestination to Life is the everlasting purpose of God, whereby (before the foundations of the world were laid) he hath constantly decreed . . . to deliver from curse and damnation those whom he hath chosen."[14] The *Westminster Confession* followed Calvin's thinking even more completely, making explicit both sides of double predestination. "By the decree of God, for the manifestation of his glory," the *Confession* stated, "some men and angels are predestinated unto everlasting life; and others foreordained to everlasting death." Also following Paul and Augustine, "Those of mankind that are predestinated unto life, God, before the foundation of the world was laid . . . hath chosen . . . out of his mere free grace and love, without any foresight of faith or good works." And what of everyone else? "The rest of mankind God was pleased . . . to pass by, and to ordain them to dishonor and wrath for their sin, to the praise of his glorious justice."[15]

The depraved nature of humans, resulting from the Fall, likewise bore implications for why humans exist in the first place and therefore what our purpose in living is, questions just as fundamental as what happens to us after we cease to exist. Numerous passages in the Hebrew Bible make clear that the creation—all of it—stands as a glory to God the creator. The New Testament repeatedly expresses the same theme. But why are *humans*, having been created only then to have fallen, enjoined to engage in this glorification? According to Calvin, glorifying God is the only purpose fallen man has left. Before Adam's sin, "Scripture attributed nothing else to him than that he had been created in the image of God." And afterward? "What, therefore, now remains for man, bare and destitute of all glory, but to recognize God for whose beneficence he could not be grateful when he abounded with the riches of his grace"—that is, before the Fall—"and at least, by confessing his own poverty, to glorify him in whom he did not previously glory."[16] The image of all creation as a theater of God's glory became a central theme in Calvinist theology.

And what, then, is the purpose of humans' existence? According to the *Westminster Confession*, "God, the great Creator of all things, doth uphold, direct, dispose, and govern all creatures, actions, and things, from the greatest to the least . . . to the praise of the glory of his wisdom, power, justice, goodness, and mercy."[17] The *Westminster Larger Catechism*, the instructional set of questions and answers written in 1646–1647 by the group of Puritan clergy who also drafted the *Westminster Confession*, followed the same line of thought. The *Catechism* begins by asking, "What is the chief and highest end of man?" The stated answer: "to glorifie God, and fully to enjoy him for ever."[18]

Calvin's ideas of depravity, predestination, and the purpose of human existence spread rapidly within the expanding Protestant world. With the publication in 1563 of the *Thirty-nine Articles*, laying out the basic tenets of Anglican belief, orthodox Calvinist theology officially prevailed within the Church of England. These ideas achieved their peak of popular influence in England in the 1640s with the Puritan victory in the English Civil War and then in the 1650s under the Puritan Commonwealth led by Oliver Cromwell. In Scotland,

Calvinists—"Presbyterians" because of their form of church governance—dominated the church beginning in 1560.

Over time, however, questions arose even among the committed faithful. Not surprisingly, the doctrine of predestination was a particular focus of concern. By the early seventeenth century, Holland had become a center of dispute over predestination among Protestant theologians. The key figure at the outset of these debates was a Dutch clergyman named Jacob Arminius, and in time "Arminian" became an all-purpose label for non-Calvinist Protestant thinking. An international Protestant synod in 1619 reaffirmed the orthodox Calvinist position, but still the discomfort festered. In England, the disagreement persisted until the Puritan ascendancy at midcentury laid it to rest. But following the collapse of the Commonwealth and restoration of the monarchy, in 1660, the tide moved rapidly in the opposite direction. From there, the movement away from orthodox Calvinist thinking in the English-speaking Protestant world was a rolling phenomenon, gaining most momentum in England in the latter half of the seventeenth century, in Scotland in the early to middle decades of the eighteenth, and in America in the latter half of the eighteenth. Importantly for the development of what became the discipline of economics, in Scotland the dispute was at its most contentious just as Adam Smith, David Hume, and their contemporaries were in their early years and forming their view of the world.

Following England's Glorious Revolution, in 1688, the new monarchs moved promptly to reshape not only the country's politics but also its religious landscape. William and Mary's appointments within the Church of England, beginning with John Tillotson as Archbishop of Canterbury, officially gave English Protestantism a more tolerant and theologically liberal face. In contrast to any firm commitment to Calvinist orthodoxy, Tillotson and the other new ecclesiastical office-holders, while clearly Protestants, mostly shared a broad, even lenient, stance on doctrine—hence their common label Latitudinarians (in their own day, "Latitude Men"). Since the Restoration, the upper levels of the Church of England had been becoming ever more Arminian. With Tillotson's appointment, anti-predestinarian thinking found clear expression at the apex of the church hierarchy.

The progress of the Enlightenment—the "Age of Reason"—provided further reinforcement. More than anyone else, the Englishman who embodied the new Enlightenment thinking during the years leading up to the Glorious Revolution and then in its immediate aftermath was John Locke. Locke was both a philosopher and an active participant in the practical political debates of his time, but he was also a committed Christian and he took a direct interest in religious matters and in the theology of the English church. In 1695 he published a book titled *The Reasonableness of Christianity as Delivered in the Scriptures*. In it, as in his earlier work, he emphasized the importance of reason as the distinguishing capacity of humans. But he also highlighted the role of God as the world's creator, and as his title suggested, he forcefully defended the compatibility of reason and religion. He also expressed what, to some, seemed a new, more benign view of the divine: "God had, by the light of reason, revealed to all mankind, who would make use of that light, that he was good and merciful."[19]

These views in turn led Locke to reject the Calvinist doctrines of human depravity and of salvation based on God's grace granted only to the elect. The same spark of the divine nature, and the same divinely bestowed knowledge that made someone a man, he argued, also showed him the path that as a man he was obliged to follow. Invoking an image that in time became commonplace in Enlightenment-inspired religious discussion, Locke referred to man's reasoning power as a candle—in this case, a candle offered to him by God. It was up to the individual whether to use it or not. "He that made use of this candle of the Lord, so far as to find out what was his duty, could not miss to find also the way to reconciliation and foregiveness."[20] In contrast to the orthodox Calvinist view that only the elect can achieve faith, the essential implication was that because God gave *all* men and women reason, all have it within their power to find their way to achieve salvation.

Another key underpinning of the movement away from orthodox Calvinist thinking was Newtonian science. A deeply religious man, Newton had conceived his *Principia Mathematica*, published just before the Glorious Revolution, as contributing to man's knowledge not only of the physical universe but also the God who had created it. Newton's work taught people to believe that the behavior of the universe was regular, governed by laws that are knowable, and that the goal of science was to gain knowledge of those laws. But believing that the universe is systematic and accessible to human understanding stood in tension to any claim that God exercised his sovereignty in a purely arbitrary way. It therefore ran against the grain of such orthodox Calvinist notions of salvation as "unconditional election"—that is, the exercise of God's sovereignty according to no more than his own act of grace, not given in respect of any merit or other understandable characteristic of the individual who received it. A series of public lectures established by the distinguished scientist Robert Boyle (best known today for the law he discovered relating the pressure exerted by a confined gas to the volume of the container that confines it) prominently brought together English scientists and theologians, in the period following the

Glorious Revolution, to promote this new effort to bring scientific thinking to bear on our understanding of God and the
nature of God's creation.

Against the background of these strong intellectual cur-
rents, and in the political climate of the Glorious Revolution
as well, English Protestant theologians continued to challenge
orthodox Calvinist doctrines. A more specific aspect of this
inquiry was the perceived tension between predestination, as
Calvin had preached the doctrine and his followers had elaborated it, and individual morality. If men and women know
that they are predestined either to be saved or not, and that
God's choice regarding their individual spiritual fate has been
made before they were born (more than that, before the world
existed), what incentive is left to motivate them to live moral
lives? And if God's choice was instead to damn them, what
would that imply about the nature of God?

This kind of non- and even anti-predestinarian thinking became both more widespread and more open after the
Glorious Revolution, especially once the new monarchs
appointed John Tillotson as Archbishop of Canterbury. Now
it was the clerical head of the Church of England himself who
was openly challenging orthodox Calvinist belief. Tillotson
rejected the orthodox Calvinist view of depravity. It was true,
he acknowledged, "that the nature of men is sadly corrupted
and depraved; but not so bad as by vicious practices and habits
it may be made." He went on, "It is a great mistake to argue
the common condition of all mankind, from the descriptions
that are given in the scripture of the worst of men." Moreover,
as Locke likewise argued, most people have the capacity to
understand what kind of life they should seek to lead. Even
those not yet convinced of religion "are not equally devoid of
a sense of God, and spiritual things"; they are "very capable of

persuasion."[21] It was this persuasion that Tillotson saw as the church's purpose. By contrast, the doctrines of depravity and predestination took away any reason for even attempting it.

Tillotson saw the need for human effort *and* for divine grace together, for an individual to achieve salvation: without grace, the effort is doomed to failure. "We affirm the necessity of God's grace hereto," he confirmed, but along with it "the necessity of our co-operating with the grace of God." Human choice and action—cooperation, as Tillotson put it—were not just possible but *necessary*. Citing both Paul and the prophets, he boldly told his listeners, "*Work out your own salvation; repent and turn yourselves from all your evil ways; make ye new hearts and new spirits.*" To him, these were all metaphors for persuading people that "we may and ought to do something toward repentance and conversion." In contrast to the Calvinist view of depravity and predestination, "We say that without the powerful excitation and aid of God's grace, no man can repent and turn to God; but we say likewise, that God cannot be properly said to *aid* and *assist* those who do nothing themselves."[22]

Tillotson died suddenly, in the fall of 1694, after leading the Church of England for only three and a half years. But his ideas about the essential importance of human agency, issuing from his position of authority within the church, long outlived him, and his writings continued to be read for decades after his death. Locke's tract on the *Reasonableness of Christianity*, published just the next year, was a further part of this attack on the Calvinist doctrines of depravity and predestination. Locke acknowledged the centrality to Christianity of the biblical story of the Fall, but he rejected outright the claim that Adam and Eve's failing contaminated all humans forevermore. The lasting outcome of the Fall was not the depravity

of Adam and all of his descendants, but simply their physical mortality. If the death to which Adam was condemned
"meant the corruption of human nature in his posterity," he
wrote, "'tis strange, that the New Testament should not any
where take notice of it."[23]

The end point of Locke's argument, like Tillotson's, was
that since mankind is *not* depraved, and humans *can* choose
to accept God's grace, and their behavior *is* effective for their
salvation, individual morality therefore matters.[24] As the eighteenth century began, this emphasis on the importance of
moral behavior—and the ability of not just the elect but all
men and women to choose to act morally—spread rapidly
among the Church of England's clergy. As the century went on,
the rejection of depravity and predestination, and in parallel
the emphasis on moral behavior and the free will to choose it,
became increasingly direct and explicit. In a widely read treatise
of 1740, the prominent theologian John Taylor argued forcefully
that the Calvinist doctrine of original sin was not just incorrect
but inconsistent with accepted biblical teachings about God's
goodness and justice—and, moreover, that the idea of depravity imputed from the Fall makes God the author of sin, in that
God has then sent his creatures into the world with insuper-
ably sinful inclinations. Taking phrases from the *Westminster
Confession*, but turning them to the opposite conclusion, Taylor
wrote, "If all Men are by Nature utterly indisposed, disabled,
and . . . wholly inclined to all Evil," then "no Man is obliged to
attempt the Reformation of the World, nor any, except Adam,
blameable for whatever Wickedness is in it."[25]

These challenges to belief in depravity and predestination,
increasingly explicit as English theologians moved forward
from Tillotson to Taylor, also bore implications for God's inten-
tions for humanity. No one questioned that man's existence

glorified God or even that, in Calvin's by-then famous phrase, the entire universe was a theater of God's glory. But increasingly, the assumption underlying the movement away from belief in orthodox ideas of depravity and predestination was that God's aims with respect to mankind had a further, more benign dimension: God *intended* the men and women he created to enjoy happiness and well-being, and in more than the mere sense that participating in glorifying God should of course make them happy.

Samuel Clarke, a theologian and philosopher who in 1704–1705 had paved new ground in natural theology with his Boyle Lectures, spoke frequently on divinely intended human happiness. In the sermons he went on to deliver during his twenty-year tenure, from 1709 until his death in 1729, as rector of the church of St. James's, Westminster (Isaac Newton served on the St. James's vestry during part of this period), Clarke saw human happiness as a deliberate part of the purpose behind God's creation of the world. The uniform intention of all God's commandments, he stated, was that "they always tend to the same regular End, the Order and Happiness of the whole Creation."[26] Clarke was explicit that this benevolence on the part of the creator plainly contradicted the orthodox doctrines of depravity and predestination. The universal happiness of "all reasonable Creatures," he thought, stemmed "from their acting according to that Nature which God has given them."[27] But if humans' nature led to happiness, that nature could not be one of depravity that inevitably sunk them in sin and misery.

The logical train of thought running from God's benevolence to the intent for human happiness, and hence to our obligation to delight in the happiness of our fellow creatures, was influential beyond the scope of religious thinking. In 1731 John Gay, a philosopher and Anglican priest teaching at Cambridge (and a cousin of the John Gay who wrote *The Beggar's Opera*), published his "Preliminary Dissertation concerning the Fundamental Principle of Virtue or Morality," in which he argued that because the happiness of mankind is willed by God, humans are obliged to act so as to maximize the happiness of their fellow creatures. "It is evident from the Nature of God," Gay wrote, that "he could have no other Design in creating Mankind than their Happiness."[28] Before the century was out, Gay's treatise had become one of the foundational texts of the utilitarian philosophy of seeking the greatest happiness for the greatest number, as later developed by such intellectual giants as Jeremy Bentham and, in the nineteenth century, John Stuart Mill.

With some lag in time, these same themes of the benevolence of God, and therefore the inherent goodness of men and women endowed by God with the power of reason, took hold in Scotland as well. So too (especially under the influence of Francis Hutcheson at the university in Glasgow) did the new emphasis on the importance of individual virtue and morality, centered on human choice and agency. While the first led to a weakening of the Scottish clergy's belief in depravity, the second led many thoughtful people to even greater discomfort with the orthodox Calvinist doctrine of predestination.

By the 1730s, when David Hume was still a young man and Adam Smith just a youth, a liberal-thinking group of self-labeled "Moderates" had emerged as the faction within the Church of Scotland most aligned with Enlightenment ideas. By the 1740s, a wide gulf had developed between these more liberal thinkers, who pointedly ignored the Calvinist doctrines of the *Westminster Confession*, and their more traditionally minded fellow clergy. Intellectually protégés of Smith's favorite professor Francis Hutcheson, and in many cases his actual students, the Moderate clergy embraced their teacher's ideas of an inborn moral sense, which likewise ran against the grain of orthodox thinking centered on depravity and predestination. In time they also developed close ties to Hume, Smith, and other secular thinkers of the Scottish Enlightenment. As time passed, the Moderates came to occupy the most significant positions within the Church of Scotland, as well as many university appointments over which the church exerted influence if not outright control. The most prominent among them was William Robertson, a historian and a personal friend to both Smith and Hume, who became principal (president) of the University of Edinburgh in 1762; from 1763 on Robertson was also frequently the moderator of the church's General Assembly. It was this group's views that Smith and Hume heard from friends in the clergy with whom they regularly associated.

4   Lasting Influences

The religious ideas that Adam Smith, David Hume, and their contemporaries imbibed from the Scottish Moderates and English Latitudinarians—the natural goodness of man in contrast to inborn depravity, the central role of free human choice and action in contrast to predestination, and the design of the universe not solely for the glorification of God but to promote human happiness too—by extension carried implications for how to think about the secular world. These further, secular implications were in turn closely aligned with the key elements of the new thinking that in time produced the Smithian revolution in economics and then shaped the evolution of modern economics ever since. To be sure, recognizing the logical connection between ideas, or even sets of ideas, is not the same as establishing historical influence.[1] But not only did the transition in thinking that set the foundation for modern economics closely follow the movement away from orthodox Calvinism in time, the two shared a logical coherence as well. To a large extent, in their thinking about both philosophy and what we now call economics, Smith and his contemporaries were secularizing the essential substance of their clerical friends' theological principles.

The concept of human depravity that was central to Calvin's theology meant that men and women were not reliably
able to tell good from bad, right from wrong, or systematically
able to act on whatever differences between them they might
perceive. (Calvin referred to the "misshapen ruins" of man's
ability to distinguish good from evil.[2]) It was not much of an
extension to conclude that they were therefore also unable to
distinguish whether their actions were good or bad in wider
contexts. In the first instance, they were unlikely to understand what actions they might take would be in their own self-
interest. Responding merely to the dictates of their depraved
nature, they were even less likely to act in ways that would
systematically render others better off.

By contrast, if whatever original sin humans might bear
does not imply Calvinist depravity—more specifically, if all
men and women are endowed with reason, and if the human
character is one of inherent goodness, as both the English Latitudinarians and the Scottish Moderates argued—then men
and women *are* able both to make moral choices and to act
with virtue. A natural extension of this distinctly more optimistic but still theologically based assessment of humanity is
that men and women also have the ability to distinguish secular good from bad, including understanding their own self-
interest. Further, there is nothing in their inborn nature that
prevents them from systematically acting in ways that can,
and under the right conditions will, result in outcomes beneficial to other people as well.

The doctrine of predestination meant that it was impossible for individuals to effect, or even contribute to, their salvation. But what else that mattered to them might they then be
unable to influence? A person's incapacity to make any choice
or take any action to promote his or her ultimate spiritual

prospects bears a natural affinity to a parallel inability to make choices or take action to improve one's material well-being. Such a person's systematically acting in ways that made others better off would seem even less likely to the predestinarian way of thinking.

The view of humans as morally conscious agents, with free will and choice, instead meant that individuals *are* able to help determine whether they are saved or not. Their ultimate destiny is, at least to some significant degree, within their control. In Locke's metaphor, they have the "candle of the Lord" by which to see and then act; in Tillotson's phrase, they are able to "cooperate" in achieving their salvation. By extension to the secular realm, people not only understand what is in their own interest, they also are able to act on that understanding. And, again under the right conditions, even though driven by no more than their inborn nature they can act to improve the lives of others too.

Finally, if the sole purpose of creation is to glorify God, then human happiness per se carries no religious value and there is no reason that the world God created should be structured so as to foster it. By contrast, if human happiness— including the potential ability of each individual to achieve a moral life, and spiritual salvation once that lifetime ends—is also part of the intent of a benevolent God, then the world in which we live is one in which those ends are not just possible but likely. By extension to secular matters, human material needs and abilities are likewise such as to enable happy lives. Individual human nature, therefore, as well as human institutions, like markets, are also likely to give rise to material aspects of satisfaction.

This more optimistic view of the human character and more expansive understanding of the possibilities for human choice and human action, advanced over the prior century to supplant orthodox Calvinist thinking, formed an essential part of the worldview that Adam Smith and his contemporaries brought to their attempt to create a science of man analogous to what Newton had constructed for the physical world. Hutcheson's and Smith's ideas about human sympathy and the desire for fellow-feeling were, in effect, a secularization of the principle of Christian love (even though Hutcheson, who wrote in an explicitly religious vein as well, would certainly have been comfortable without the secularization), applied to men and women whose nature was not depraved but characterized by an innate goodness. The idea that people acting on no more than their own natural desires can nonetheless improve not only their own material lives but others' too mirrored the belief that all people, not just the elect few, can succeed in achieving a moral life. Smith's insight into the role of markets and competition in rendering what can happen into what *will* happen reflected the increasingly widespread belief that the benevolent God who created the world intended the human creatures he put in it to be happy, and therefore that God also endowed their world with the human institutions needed to channel their behavior accordingly.[3]

There is little reason to believe that these resonances between the new economic ideas and these new lines of religious thinking were a matter of conscious intent. Hume was a notorious skeptic (many regarded him as an atheist) and an avowed opponent of organized religion in any form. He publicly referred to Church of England bishops as "retainers to superstition," and his friend William Robertson, principal of Edinburgh University and also head of the Church of Scotland, thought of him as a "heathen."[4] Smith kept his religious beliefs to himself; but there is no evidence, in his writings or personal behavior, of any deep personal commitment. More likely, he was, like many Enlightenment figures—Thomas Jefferson, for example, or Benjamin Franklin—a deist. The influence of the new religious thinking on Smith's and Hume's economic ideas was hardly a product of their consciously bringing their personal religious beliefs to bear on what they thought and wrote about the subject.

Rather, these creators of modern economics lived at a time when religion was more central to their society, and more pervasive in it, than anything the Western world knows today. Especially in the wake of the Act of Union in 1707, in which Scotland had given up its independent parliament and royal court, Scottish politics and patronage revolved around the church. Intellectual life was also more integrated then. At the University of Glasgow Smith was one of only fourteen professors; the others included a professor of theology and a professor of church history. No one had yet thought of hiving off these lines of religious study into separate schools of divinity, as is the case at many universities today. The clubs and dining societies that stood at the heart of the vibrant Enlightenment culture of mid-eighteenth-century Edinburgh and Glasgow likewise brought members of the clergy together with the era's leading secular thinkers. Smith and Hume were both among the original thirty-one members of the most distinguished of these groups, the Select Society. Five of the others (including their friend Robertson) were Church of Scotland clergymen.

And religious debate was more contentious then than anything the Western world knows today. These were ideas for which men fought and many died. A hundred years earlier, on the continent, the Thirty Years' War between Catholic and Protestant forces caused as many deaths, compared to the size of Europe's population, as did World War II three

centuries later. The English Civil War, fought within the lifetime of Smith's and Hume's grandfathers—in this instance
again between Catholic sympathizers and Protestants, but
also between Calvinist and non-Calvinist Protestants—was
similarly deadly. It also led to the execution of the king and,
for eleven years, abolition of Britain's monarchy. Following
the Restoration, ongoing resistance to royal authority in both
England and Scotland was likewise often based on religious differences. In Scotland, the Jacobite Rebellion of 1745, in which
the exiled Stuart (Catholic) forces attempted to overthrow the
Hanoverian (Protestant) monarchy, took place when Smith
was twenty-two years old. Some of the fighting occurred right
outside Edinburgh.

With the controversy surrounding the movement away
from predestinarian Calvinism at its height in Scotland just as
Smith and Hume were coming to young adulthood, the new
religious ideas shaped the mindset with which they viewed the
world in which they lived and which they sought to understand and analyze. Albert Einstein, writing in 1918—three
years before he won the Nobel Prize, but after he had published his theory of general relativity—set down his thoughts
on how research scientists come up with their ideas. Einstein
chose not to limit himself to scientists, however, because in
this regard he saw them as no different from creative, thinking
human beings more generally. The greatest need, he thought,
was some way to see through complexity. To do so requires
a simplifying mechanism, a ready reference framework that
skips over distracting details to highlight what is important.
"Man seeks to form for himself," Einstein wrote, "in whatever
manner is suitable for him, a simplified and easy-to-survey
image of the world and so to overcome the world of experience by striving to replace it to some extent by this image.

This is what the painter does, and the poet, the speculative philosopher, the natural scientist, each in his own way."[5]

Einstein's notion of an "image of the world"—a worldview—that shapes an individual's thinking, especially at the frontier at which creativity confronts reality, has appealed to others as well. Joseph Schumpeter later expressed the same idea, specifically in the context of economics, as the "pre-analytic Vision" underlying an economist's thought.[6] Importantly, the image of the world that shapes a person's creative thinking is often not that person's alone. Gerald Holton, the leading late-twentieth-century authority on Einstein's own thought, interpreted it as, more likely, a commonly shared aspect of the era in which someone lives: what matters is the thinker's cultural roots, the "milieu in which he and his fellow scientists grew up," the "internal architecture of a person *or a period*."[7] In the same vein, Robert Merton, the historian of science who famously explored the intellectual atmosphere in which the English in the mid-seventeenth century founded Britain's Royal Society, referred to the "cultural soil" that encourages new ideas to emerge, and then either flourish or not.[8] Again, there is no reason to regard economics as an exception. As John Kenneth Galbraith put it, "Economic ideas are always and intimately a product of their own time and place."[9]

The addition of contemporary religious thinking to the conventional understanding of the influences acting on the economic thinking of Adam Smith and his contemporaries exhibits some parallels to the hypothesis about the origins of capitalism famously offered more than a century ago by Max Weber in his classic work *The Protestant Ethic and the Spirit of Capitalism*, but also some sharp differences.[10] Weber too emphasized the powerful influence of religious thinking outside the realm of religion narrowly defined, and Calvinist ideas about predestination

were likewise at the center of Weber's hypothesis: Knowing that
each person had been either saved or damned for all eternity—
and with no opportunity to affect that determination, which
had already been made eons before his or her birth—led Calvinist believers to seek comfort from external signs that, while
in no way causal for this purpose, might nonetheless signify
that they were among the elect. Their "existential anxiety" (a
term used by Weber and revived by the mid-twentieth-century
theologian Paul Tillich[11]) therefore led them to attach religious
value to forms of behavior, like industriousness and thrift,
which Weber argued were conducive to the ongoing search for
profit that he identified as the distinguishing feature of modern
capitalism. Moreover, Weber argued, over time these "Protestant virtues" acquired a free-standing moral value separate from
any specific theological or religious basis.

The focus of the argument here, by contrast, is not on economic behavior but *thinking* about economics—and, moreover, on the thinking of those few individuals whose principal
activity was to create new ideas and write about them. Even
more different, Adam Smith and the creators of modern economics lived not during the time Weber emphasized but a
century and more later, when belief in predestination was
under strenuous assault among English-speaking Protestants
and well in retreat. The key religious influence on their thinking was therefore not belief in predestination but the more
optimistic view of the human character and the expanded
understanding of the possibilities for human agency fostered
by the movement *away from* that belief. In this respect, the
argument here is more nearly Weber upside down.

But there is another parallel to Weber's hypothesis as
well. Weber argued at length that the economic behavior he
attributed in part to religious thinking—in his argument, to

belief in predestination—long outlived the religious beliefs
that initially fostered it. (Presumably for this reason, Weber
chose as his "ideal type," to represent the persistent commitment to thrift and industriousness, the profoundly secular Benjamin Franklin.) The same persistence, long outliving
the initial religious impulse, has likewise been evident in the
influence of the later movement away from predestinarian
belief. The worldview stemming from the new and fiercely
contended ideas about God and about the condition and pros-
pect of mankind that were under debate in Scotland in Adam
Smith's youth and young adulthood was part of the cultural
soil that enabled Smith's contribution, and that of others of
his day, to the line of thinking that in time became economics. These secular ideas have long outlived the religious controversy that initially spawned them. They have stood at the
core of economic thinking ever since, part of the worldview,
or "Vision," underpinning economists' thought process.

Thomas Kuhn explained that it is when a science is in its
infancy that its fundamental concepts and theoretical proposi-
tions are most subject to external influence. But he also argued
that intellectual disciplines often respond to outside thinking
well beyond their youth. Then, however, the influence is more
a matter of method and application.[12] Economics too has followed this pattern. Long after the fundamental influence of
religious thinking at the inception of modern economics,
even as the economy of the Western world evolved and the
questions economists asked changed along with it, the field
continued to be shaped in part by religious thinking. By then,
however, much of the fundamental conceptual underpinning of the discipline was set. What religious thinking helped

to shape, as the discipline matured, was more the empirical implementation of economic thought and its application to issues of economic policy. Nowhere has this influence been more evident than in America.

The chief economic issue under debate in the United States in the first half of the nineteenth century (leaving aside the economic aspects of slavery) was international trade. Not surprisingly, the subject became a principal focus of attention among the country's new wave of Smith-influenced economists. In contrast to Smith, in the early United States many of the leading teachers of and writers about economics *were* religiously committed men. Where Smith invoked the invisible hand of the market forces he laid out in such detail, they saw the hand of God at work—much as Newton had argued was the case in the physical world. John McVickar, who taught the first college course in economics given in America (at Columbia), was an Episcopal priest. Francis Wayland, author of the best-selling American textbook on economics before the Civil War, was a Baptist minister. Francis Bowen, author of the major competing textbook, was not ordained but was nonetheless closely associated with the Unitarian movement.

All three of these economists, whether for free trade or against, framed their arguments in explicitly religious terms. McVickar, a strong proponent of free trade, followed earlier thinkers like Montesquieu and Thomas Paine in hailing international economic relations as a route to peace among nations. Arguing that beneficial consequences of human actions occur because a benevolent God makes them so, he wrote in the 1830s, "I cannot but reverence the claims of free commerce as something *holy*, something allied to the policy of a higher power than man."[13] Even more strongly, in another work McVicar stated, "To forbid trade among nations is, therefore, a very unwise thing; but it is also a very wicked thing, for it is contrary to the will of God."[14] Wayland shared the same view and was more explicit about how the process worked: "Every man needs, for the gratification of his innocent desires, nay, for his conveniences and even necessaries, the productions of every part of the globe . . . it is evidently the will of our Creator, that but few of these objects, every one of which is necessary to the happiness of every individual, should be produced except in particular districts." Trade among nations was therefore a physical necessity. The reason, he concluded—the "final cause of all this"—was also evident: "God intended that men should live together in friendship and harmony."[15] On the other side of the debate, Francis Bowen, a protectionist (his reason for writing a textbook to compete with Wayland's was to advocate tariffs), made an analogous claim in support of protection. "By treating the human race as one great family," he warned, "we are not following, but departing from, the apparent design of Providence." In contrast to Wayland's vision of the world's oceans as a device for knitting countries together through commerce, Bowen concluded that "the Deity seems to have stamped on the features of nature and of humanity, in unmistakable characters, that nations shall remain separate and distinct, each pursuing . . . its own separate interests."[16] Unrestricted trade, he thought, upset the natural state of affairs that God had intended for the world. Whether advocating free trade or protection, American economists in the pre–Civil War period anchored their views in religious argument.

By the latter half of the nineteenth century, the Industrial Revolution was in full swing. Steam power, which in Adam Smith's day was just beginning to drive factory production, now powered not only factories on a far larger scale but railroads too. The movement of populations into urban centers had not just advanced but accelerated. Nowhere were these changes more evident than in the United States. The period following America's Civil War was a particular era of economic change, marked by both rapid population growth and the fastest increase in per capita production and living standards in the country's experience recorded before or since. Despite all this prosperity, however, many Americans had reservations about what the new economic era had brought. Most visibly, the combination of mass production and urbanization had created a new mass urban workforce. And along with it came widespread and persistent urban poverty.

Significantly for the evolution of economics, the social sciences in the United States were at this same time beginning to emulate the professionalization that these disciplines had already achieved a generation or more before in Europe, especially in Germany. In 1865 scholars from a variety of subject areas had formed the American Social Science Association. Two decades later, what had been closely allied lines of inquiry within this broad umbrella began to go their separate ways. In 1885, following the lead of the historians the year before, a group met to create the American Economic Association (AEA). In a reflection of the same movement toward intellectual professionalization, American universities were then beginning to organize their faculties into divisions and departments along subject-based lines. By 1890 the University of Chicago, Columbia University, Harvard University, Johns Hopkins University, the University of Michigan, the University of Pennsylvania, Princeton University, the University of Wisconsin, and Yale University all had recognizable departments of economics. A further expression of professionalization was the establishment of dedicated scholarly journals as outlets for new thinking. In 1886 economists at Harvard began publishing *the Quarterly Journal of Economics,* and those at Chicago followed with the *Journal of Political Economy* (still using the older name for the discipline) in 1892. Early in the new century the AEA launched its own journal, the *American Economic Review.*

This new generation of American economists were strongly non-predestinarian in their personal religious beliefs, and it showed in the direction that the discipline took under their leadership. John Bates Clark, the foremost theorist among them, expressed concern that the image of man on which economists were now basing their analysis "may or may not resemble the man whom God has created"; in his view, "the latter only is the true subject of political economy." Anticipating criticisms of economic thinking that became far more prevalent a century later (and that persist today), he complained, "The assumed man is too mechanical and too selfish to correspond with the reality." Men and women, as God created them, were human in all respects. "What is true of a laboring machine requiring only to be housed and clothed, and to be fed . . . will certainly not be altogether true of a laboring *man* in modern society."[17]

Many American economists of this period were also influenced by the Social Gospel movement then gaining momentum among America's Protestant churches in reaction to the persistence of poverty and widening economic inequality despite ongoing industrial expansion. Mirroring the central theological thrust of the Social Gospel, Clark argued that *the conditions of society* shape individuals' attitudes and behavior. Influences stemming from society as a whole, he explained, were capable of transforming individual nature. An individual man or woman became "higher and better" by being a part of a well-designed society. Best of all, under the right conditions men's "higher wants"—including the ingredients of "intellectual, aesthetic and moral growth"—could expand without bound, resulting in "a limitless outlet for productive energy." The thought had significant implications for economic theory: there was no reason to anticipate the kind of stagnant "stationary state" about which John Stuart Mill and others had theorized earlier in the century. In Clark's evaluation, the extent to which this limitless human energy is utilized was "the gauge of genuine economic progress."[18] And there were practical implications too: economic *policy*—government action—could make an important difference. "We may build a new earth out of the difficult material we have to work with," he wrote (invoking language from the biblical Book of Revelation), "and cause justice and kindness to rule in the very place where strife now holds sway." With the right guidance, "a New Jerusalem may actually rise out of the fierce contentions of the modern market. The wrath of men may praise God and his Kingdom may come, not in spite of, but by means of the contests of the economic sphere."[19]

Richard T. Ely, the leading applied policy economist of the era, and more than anyone else the person responsible for establishing the American Economic Association, likewise resisted any kind of determinism, emphasizing instead the capacity of human agency to shape not only individuals' spiritual destiny but also conditions in the material world. He too saw the economic condition of society as the outcome of human decisions and human actions. The key implication was that people bear a moral responsibility for how they and their fellow citizens live.

Drawing on his graduate training in the thinking of the German historical school, Ely suggested for this purpose a new methodology based on the use of explicit cross-country comparison as a way to gain a deeper understanding of whatever behavior was under study, as well as to introduce the possibility of deliberate ameliorative intervention. "We can observe certain regularities and tendencies in all social phenomena," he wrote. What, then, should economists conclude about these regularities? When people observed that many of the social phenomena that mattered appeared to recur regularly, year after year, "a feeling akin to fatalism arose, and some statisticians were inclined to look upon these regularities as . . . beyond the control of man." But such an attitude contradicted Ely's non-predestinarian sense of the possibilities for human agency. A deeper inquiry, he pointed out, revealed differences in these regularities between one country and another. And still further analysis showed that these differences "could be brought about by the action of man."[20] There were few or no universal economic regularities, valid at all times and in all places. Economic behavior, like every other aspect of human life, was conditional on the prevailing social arrangements.

What social arrangements to pursue, and therefore which economic policies to implement, are questions that have dominated the discipline ever since. The great majority of articles published in the field's scholarly journals today motivate whatever question is under study by pointing to its bearing on economic policy, or conclude by drawing policy implications from the analysis presented, or both. This pattern is even more prevalent, with the policy content of the analysis bulking still larger, in books about economics aimed at a broad public audience. The educated public today expects discussion of economics to be about public policy. Thanks in no small part to Clark and Ely, it largely is.

Debates not only over specific economic policies but also about what role government should play more generally, in the economy as well as in the society broadly, have continued to frame the field's agenda. Here too, the influence of religious thinking has been at work throughout, especially in America. Early in the twentieth century, the legacy of the Social Gospel movement stood behind Franklin Roosevelt's New Deal. More conservative groups within American Protestantism, grounded in different theological beliefs, led the opposition to it. At midcentury, under the impetus of the existential threat posed by world Communism, the coming together of religious conservatism, centered in America's evangelical churches, and economic conservatism, which drew new energy from the infusion of the libertarian thinking of the Austrian Friedrich von Hayek, shaped much of the economic debate in the public sphere. In time this union of conservatisms proved highly influential within the academic economic profession as well.

Today, the influence of religious thinking on economic thinking is most readily visible in America's public conversation about economics and the country's debate over economic policy. Members of evangelical Protestant denominations in particular hold sharply different views on many questions of economic policy than Americans on average, including members of the country's mainline Protestant denominations. These differences are even greater among evangelical denominations considered "traditionalist." Similar differences appear in responses to surveys focusing not on economic policy but on underlying presumptions about how the economy works: whether individual economic success is mostly a matter of luck or hard work, or whether the poor are trapped in their poverty.

Such religiously grounded differences in people's world-view also go a long way toward explaining the puzzle, much discussed in the empirical political science literature,[21] of why so many Americans vote in ways apparently contrary to their economic self-interest. Why, for example, do so many low-income voters oppose taxes that they would never have to pay and benefit programs on which they rely? Why do so many people living in areas blighted by industrial waste and pollution oppose regulation or other policies to prevent such damage, or efforts to clean up what has occurred in the past? The strong correlation between people's views on such matters and either their religious affiliations or their individual religious beliefs suggests that any effort to understand these observed patterns without taking account of the role of religious ideas in shaping people's thinking on matters of economics is, at best, seriously incomplete.

Economics today is still about human choices and the possibilities that they present. This was the central issue under contention in the controversy over predestinarian Calvinism that was under such hot debate in Adam Smith's early years. That debate strongly influenced Smith's worldview, and his worldview in turn shaped his economic thinking.

This influence remains with us today. The First Fundamental Welfare Theorem, the basis for which Smith established in *The Wealth of Nations*, still stands at the heart of economists' analytical apparatus. Economic choices—the decisions and actions of households and firms—remain the essential stuff of both economic theory and empirical work. The more expansive, and more optimistic, view of human agency and human

possibilities that Smith and Hume embodied in their writings
remains ours as well.

Economics has been, since its inception, a child of the
Enlightenment, with all of the optimism about the human
enterprise that that epochal movement entailed. Religious
thinking has been part of this story throughout.

Notes

Introduction

1. Morgan, *Birth of the Republic*, 51.

2. Keynes, *General Theory*, 383.

3. Friedman, *Religion and the Rise of Capitalism*. Parts of this lecture draw on that work.

4. Kuhn, "History of Science," 109, 118–119.

5. Brunner, "Religion and the Social Order"; Brunner, "Perception of Man."

6. Brunner, "Conversation with a Monetarist," 181, 182.

7. For an overview of Zwingli's life and thought, see Gordon, *Zwingli*.

8. See, for example, Stephens, "The Place of Predestination in Zwingli and Bucer," on Zwingli's quite different view of predestination.

9. See Campi, "The Reformation in Zurich," and Gordon, *The Swiss Reformation*, ch. 2.

Chapter 1

1. See Pocock, *Machiavellian Moment*, part 3.

2. See, for example, Whatmore, "Luxury, Commerce, and the Rise of Political Economy," and Slack, *Invention of Improvement*, chs. 5–6.

3. MacCulloch, *The Reformation*, 643.

4. For a useful overview, see Brooke, *Philosophic Pride*, ch. 5.

5. As a practical matter even the medieval church tolerated interest on loans other than to individuals, such as loans to the king or for commercial purposes.

6. Hume, "Of the Balance of Trade," in *Essays*, 308–326.

7. Hume, "Of the Jealousy of Trade," in *Essays*, 327–331.

8. Jean Bodin, a sixteenth-century French political philosopher, offered an earlier expression of a similar idea; Bodin, *Six Bookes*, 660.

9. Smith, *Wealth of Nations*, 96, 99.

Chapter 2

1. For Smith's biography, see Ross, *Life of Adam Smith*, and Phillipson, *Adam Smith*.

2. See, for example, Skinner, "Adam Smith: The French Connection," and many of the references cited there.

3. Phillipson, *Adam Smith*, 194.

4. Smith, letter to David Hume, July 5, 1764, in *Correspondence of Adam Smith*, 102.

5. Keynes, *End of Laissez-Faire*, 12.

6. Smith, *Wealth of Nations*, 341.

7. Smith, 341.

8. Smith, 13.

9. Smith, 26–27.

10. Smith, 343.

11. Hume, *Treatise of Human Nature*, 316; Smith, *Wealth of Nations*, 341.

12. Smith, 429, 660.

13. Smith, 267.

14. Smith, 842, 725, 888–891, 893.

15. Smith, 540, 606, 343.

16. Winch, "Introduction," in Ricardo, *Principles of Political Economy and Taxation*, vii.

Chapter 3

1. Nicole, "Of Charity and Self-Love." As an undergraduate at Glasgow, Smith had studied the logic textbook coauthored by Pierre Nicole and Antoine Arnoud.

2. On the influence of Stoicism on Smith's thinking, see Brown, *Adam Smith's Discourse*, and Force, *Self-Interest before Adam Smith*, esp. chs. 2, 3.

3. See Viner, "Adam Smith and Laissez Faire," 117.

4. Smith, *Wealth of Nations*, 75; emphasis added.

5. Augustine, *City of God against the Pagans*, 555–556.

6. Calvin, *Institutes of the Christian Religion*, 36, 251.

7. Article IX, *Thirty-nine Articles*, in Leith, *Creeds of the Churches*, 269.

8. Chapter VI, Articles I, III, and IV, *Westminster Confession*, in Leith, 201.

9. Romans 11:1–6. (Here and below, all Bible translations are the King James Version. In this case, however, the meaning is perhaps easier to read in the New Revised Version: "there is a remnant, chosen by grace . . . if it is by grace, it is no longer on the basis of works; otherwise grace would no longer be grace.")

10. Ephesians 2:8–9. See also Galatians 2:16.

11. Ephesians 1:4–6.

12. Augustine, *Treatise on the Gift of Perseverance*, 539–540.

13. Calvin, *Institutes of the Christian Religion*, 921, 926, 931. For a concise overview of the historical development of predestinarian doctrine, see Thuesen, *Predestination*, ch. 1.

14. Article XVII, *Thirty-nine Articles*, in Leith, *Creeds of the Churches*, 272.

15. Chapter III, Articles III–VII, *Westminster Confession*, in Leith, 198–199.

16. Calvin, *Institutes of the Christian Religion*, 256.

17. Chapter V, Article I, *Westminster Confession*, in Leith, *Creeds of the Churches*, 200.

18. *Westminster Larger Catechism*, 3.

19. Locke, *The Reasonableness of Christianity*, in *Works*, vol. 6, 133.

20. Locke, 133.

21. Tillotson, "Of the Nature of Regeneration," in *Works*, vol. 5, 306–307.

22. Tillotson, 308–309, 320; italics in the original.

23. Locke, *Reasonableness of Christianity*, in *Works*, vol. 6, 7.

24. See, for example, Spellman, "Locke and the Latitudinarian Perspective on Original Sin," 215–228.

25. Taylor, *Scripture Doctrine of Original Sin*, 169.

26. Clarke, "Sermon VII: Of the Immutability of God," in *Sermons*, 152.

27. Clarke, "Sermon XIII: Of the Wisdom of God," in *Sermons*, 298.

28. Gay, "Preliminary Dissertation," xix.

Chapter 4

1. See the useful discussion in Brown, *The Nature of Social Laws*, 18–23.

2. Calvin, *Institutes of the Christian Religion*, 270.

3. For a different, but not contradictory, view of the relationship between these religious ideas and Adam Smith's work, see Waterman, "Economics as Theology," 907–921.

4. Robertson, Letter to Margaret Hepburn, f. 235r.

5. Einstein, "Motive des Forchens" [Principles of Research]; translation from Holton, "On Einstein's *Weltbild*," 3.

6. Schumpeter, *History of Economic Analysis*, 41; uppercase V in the original.

7. Holton, "Einstein and the Cultural Roots of Modern Science," 1; Holton, "On Einstein's *Weltbild*," 1, emphasis added.

8. Merton, *Science, Technology and Society*, 238.

9. Galbraith, *Economics in Perspective*, 1.

10. Weber, *Protestant Ethic and the Spirit of Capitalism*.

11. Tillich, *Courage to Be*, esp. 40–54.

12. Kuhn, *History of Science*, 118–119.

13. McVickar, *Introductory Lecture*, 34.

14. McVickar, *First Lessons*, 31.

15. Wayland, *Elements of Political Economy*, 88–90.

16. *Bowen, Principles of Political Economy*, 473.

17. Clark, *Philosophy of Wealth*, 34–35.

18. Clark, 42, 40, 95.

19. Clark, *Social Justice Without Socialism*, 47–48. The reference is to Revelation 21:1–2.

20. Ely, *Introduction to Political Economy*, 126–127.

21. See, for example, Mettler, *The Government-Citizen Disconnect*. For a widely discussed popular treatment, see Frank, *What's the Matter with Kansas?*; also, Bartels, "What's the Matter with *What's the Matter with Kansas?*"

Bibliography

Augustine. *The City of God against the Pagans*. Cambridge: Cambridge University Press, 1998.

Augustine. *A Treatise on the Gift of Perseverance*. In *A Select Library of the Nicene and Post-Nicene Fathers of the Christian Church*. New York: Charles Scribner's Sons, 1908.

Bartels, Larry M. "What's the Matter with *What's the Matter with Kansas?*" *Quarterly Journal of Political Science* 1 (April 2006): 201–226.

Bodin, Jean. *The Six Bookes of a Commonweale*. Cambridge, MA: Harvard University Press, 1962.

Bowen, Francis. *The Principles of Political Economy: Applied to the Condition, the Resources, and the Institutions of the American People*. Boston: Little, Brown, 1856.

Brooke, Christopher. *Philosophic Pride: Stoicism and Political Thought from Lipsius to Rousseau*. Princeton: Princeton University Press, 2012.

Brown, Robert. *The Nature of Social Laws: Machiavelli to Mill*. Cambridge: Cambridge University Press, 1984.

Brown, Vivienne. *Adam Smith's Discourse: Canonicity, Commerce and Conscience*. London: Routledge, 1994.

Brunner, Karl. "Conversation with a Monetarist." In *Conversations with Economists: New Classical Economists and Opponents Speak Out on the Current Controversy in Macroeconomics*, edited by Arjo Klamer, 179–199. Totowa, NJ: Rowman & Allanheld, 1984.

Brunner, Karl. "The Perception of Man and the Conception of 'Society': Two Approaches to Understand Society." *Economic Inquiry* 25 (July 1987): 367–388.

Brunner, Karl. "Religion and the Social Order." Paper presented at the Southern Economic Association annual meeting, November 1987, and the Interlaken Seminar on Analysis and Ideology, May 1988.

Calvin, John. *Institutes of the Christian Religion*. 2 vols. Louisville: Westminster John Knox Press, 1960.

Campi, Emidio. "The Reformation in Zurich." In *A Companion to the Swiss Reformation*, edited by Amy Nelson Burnett and Emidio Campi, 59–125. Leiden: Brill, 2016.

Cantillon, Richard. *Essay on the Nature of Trade in General*. Indianapolis: Liberty Fund, 2015.

Clark, John Bates. *The Philosophy of Wealth: Economic Principles Newly Formulated*. Boston: Ginn & Company, 1894.

Clark, John Bates. *Social Justice Without Socialism*. Boston: Houghton Mifflin, 1914.

Clarke, Samuel. *Sermons on the Following Subjects, Viz: Of Faith in God. Of the Unity of God. Of the Eternity of God. Of the Spirituality of God. Of the Immutability of God. Of the Omnipresence of God. Of the Omnipotence of God. Of the Omniscience of God. Of the Wisdom of God. Of the Goodness of God. Of the Patience of God. Of the Justice of God*. London: W. Botham, 1730.

Einstein, Albert. "Motive des Forchens" [Principles of Research]. In *Zu Max Plancks sechzigstem Geburtstag. Ansprachen, gehalten am 26 April 1918 in der deutschen physikalischen Gesellschaft*, edited by Emil Warburg, 29–32. Karlsruhe: C. F. Mueller, 1918.

Ely, Richard T. *An Introduction to Political Economy*. New York: Chautauqua Press, 1889.

Force, Pierre. *Self-Interest before Adam Smith: A Genealogy of Economic Science*. Cambridge: Cambridge University Press, 2003.

Frank, Thomas. *What's the Matter with Kansas? How Conservatives Won the Heart of America*. New York: Metropolitan Books, 2004.

Friedman, Benjamin M. *Religion and the Rise of Capitalism*. New York: Alfred A. Knopf, 2021.

Galbraith, John Kenneth, *Economics in Perspective: A Critical History*. Boston: Houghton Mifflin, 1987.

Gay, John. "Preliminary Dissertation Concerning the Fundamental Principle of Virtue or Morality." In William King, *An Essay on the Origin of Evil*, xi–xx. London: W. Thurlbourn, 1731.

Gordon, Bruce. *The Swiss Reformation*. Manchester: Manchester University Press, 2002.

Gordon, Bruce. *Zwingli: God's Armed Prophet*. New Haven, CT: Yale University Press, 2021.

Holton, Gerald. "Einstein and the Cultural Roots of Modern Science." *Daedalus* 127, no. 1, Science in Culture (Winter 1998): 1–44.

Holton, Gerald. "On Einstein's *Weltbild*." Unpublished manuscript.

The Humble Advice Of the Assembly Of Divines, Now by Authority of Parliament sitting at Westminster, Concerning A Larger Catechism. London: Robert Bostock, 1648. [Referred to as *Westminster Larger Catechism* in the text and notes.]

Hume, David. *Essays: Moral, Political and Literary*. Edited by Eugene F. Miller. Indianapolis: Liberty Fund, 1987.

Hume, David. *A Treatise of Human Nature*. Edited by David Fate Norton and Mary J. Norton. 2 vols. Oxford: Oxford University Press, 2007.

Keynes, John Maynard. *The End of Laissez-Faire*. London: Hogarth Press, 1926.

Keynes, John Maynard. *The General Theory of Employment, Interest, and Money*. New York: Harcourt, Brace & World, 1936.

Kuhn, Thomas. "The History of Science." In *The Essential Tension: Selected Studies in Scientific Tradition and Change*, 105–126. Chicago: University of Chicago Press, 1977.

Leith, John H., ed. *Creeds of the Churches: A Reader in Christian Doctrine from the Bible to the Present*. Louisville: John Knox Press, 1982.

Locke, John. *The Works of John Locke in Nine Volumes*. 9 vols. London: C. and J. Riving, 1824.

MacCulloch, Diarmaid. *The Reformation: A History*. New York: Viking, 2003.

Mandeville, Bernard. *The Fable of the Bees. Or, Private Vices, Publick Benefits*. 2 vols. Oxford: Clarendon Press, 1924.

McVickar, John. *First Lessons in Political Economy*. Albany, NY: Common School Depository, 1837.

McVickar, John. *Introductory Lecture to a Course of Political Economy*. London: John Miller, 1830.

Merton, Robert K. *Science, Technology and Society in Seventeenth-Century England*. New York: H. Fertig, 1970 (1938).

Mettler, Suzanne. *The Government-Citizen Disconnect*. New York: Russell Sage Foundation, 2018.

Morgan, Edmund S. *The Birth of the Republic: 1763–89*. 4th ed. Chicago: University of Chicago Press, 2013.

Nicole, Pierre. "Of Charity and Self-Love." In *Moral Essays*, vol. 3, 123–176. London: Printed for R. Bentley and M. Magnes, 1680.

Phillipson, Nicholas. *Adam Smith: An Enlightened Life*. New Haven, CT: Yale University Press, 2010.

Pocock, J. G. A. *The Machiavellian Moment: Florentine Political Thought and the Atlantic Republican Tradition*. Princeton: Princeton University Press, 1975.

Ricardo, David. *The Principles of Political Economy and Taxation*. London: J. M. Dent, 1973.

Robertson, William. Letter to Margaret Hepburn, February 20, 1759. National Library of Scotland, MS 16711, ff. 234–236.

Ross, Ian Simpson. *The Life of Adam Smith*. Oxford: Oxford University Press, 2010.

Schumpeter, Joseph A. *History of Economic Analysis*. New York: Oxford University Press, 1954.

Skinner, Andrew S. "Adam Smith: The French Connection." University of Glasgow Business School, Working Paper 9703 (1997).

Slack, Paul. *The Invention of Improvement: Information and Material Progress in Seventeenth-Century England*. Oxford: Oxford University Press, 2015.

Smith, Adam. *The Correspondence of Adam Smith*. Edited by E. C. Mossner and I. S. Ross. Oxford: Clarendon Press, 1987.

Smith, Adam. *An Inquiry into the Nature and Causes of the Wealth of Nations*. 2 vols. Oxford: Oxford University Press, 1976.

Smith, Adam. *The Theory of Moral Sentiments*. Oxford: Oxford University Press, 1976.

Spellman, W. M. "Locke and the Latitudinarian Perspective on Original Sin." *Revue Internationale de Philosophie* 42 (January 1988): 215–228.

Stephens, William Peter. "The Place of Predestination in Zwingli and Bucer." *Zwingliana* 19, no. 1 (1991): 393–410.

Taylor, John. *The Scripture Doctrine of Original Sin Proposed to Free and Candid Examination*. London: J. Waugh, 1750.

Thuesen, Peter J. *Predestination: The American Career of a Contentious Doctrine*. Oxford: Oxford University Press, 2009.

Tillich, Paul. *The Courage to Be*. New Haven, CT: Yale University Press, 2000.

Tillotson, John. *The Works of the Most Reverend Dr John Tillotson, Late Lord Archbishop of Canterbury, in ten volumes*. Edinburgh: Wal. Ruddiman & Company, 1772.

Viner, Jacob. "Adam Smith and Laissez Faire." *Journal of Political Economy* 35 (April 1927): 198–232.

Waterman, A. M. C. "Economics as Theology: Adam Smith's *Wealth of Nations.*" *Southern Economic Journal* 68 (April 2002): 907–921.

Wayland, Francis. *The Elements of Political Economy*. New York: Leavitt, Lord & Company, 1837.

Weber, Max. *The Protestant Ethic and the Spirit of Capitalism*. New York: Routledge, 2005.

Whatmore, Richard. "Luxury, Commerce, and the Rise of Political Economy." In *The Oxford Handbook of British Philosophy in the Eighteenth Century*, edited by James A. Harris, 270–288. Oxford: Oxford University Press, 2013.

Index

Industrial Revolution, 23, 59

Industriousness, religious value attached to, 56

Interest on loans, 12, 68n5

Interlaken Seminar on Analysis and Ideology, 3–4

International trade
debate over, in United States, 58–59
Hume's theory of, 13–14

"Invisible hand" metaphor, 22, 30, 58

Jacobite Rebellion of 1745, 54

Jefferson, Thomas, 53

Johns Hopkins University, 60

Jordan, Thomas, 3

Journal of Monetary Economics, 3

Journal of Money, Credit and Banking, 3

Journal of Political Economy, 61

Keynes, John Maynard, 1

Knight, Frank, 4

Konstanz Seminar on Monetary Theory and Policy, 3

Kuhn, Thomas, 2, 57

Latitudinarians ("Latitude Men"), 40, 49, 50

Loans, interest on, 12, 68n5

Locke, John
Calvinist doctrines rejected by, 40–41, 43, 44
on humans as morally conscious agents, 51

Louis XIV (king of France), 11, 12

Luther, Martin, 4, 32, 33

Mandeville, Bernard, 22, 23, 29

Market competition, self-interest and, 20–23

Marshall, Alfred, 20

Mass production, 60

McVickar, John, 58–59

Mercantilism, Adam Smith's opposition to, 23–25

Merton, Robert, 55

Mesot, Joel, 4

Mill, John Stuart, 46, 62

Moderates, Scottish, 46–47, 49, 50

Monopolies, 12, 13

Montesquieu (Charles Louis de Secondat), 58

Morality
emphasis on free will and, 44, 50–51
predestination and, 42

Morgan, Edmund, 1

New Deal, Social Gospel movement and, 64

New Testament, 35, 37, 44

Newton, Isaac, 16, 30, 41, 45, 52, 58

Newtonian science
influence on Adam Smith's thinking, 30
movement away from Orthodox Calvinism and, 41–42

Nicole, Pierre, 22, 23, 29